Innovative Business Development

Innovative Business Development

Implementing Transformation From Within

Yaron Flint

BEP

BUSINESS EXPERT PRESS

Leader in applied, concise business books

First published in 2024 by
Business Expert Press, LLC
222 East 46th Street, New York, NY 10017
www.businessexpertpress.com

ISBN-13: 978-1-63742-706-4 (paperback)
ISBN-13: 978-1-63742-707-1 (e-book)

Business Expert Press Service Systems and Innovation for Business and Society Collection

First edition: 2024

10 9 8 7 6 5 4 3 2 1

Description

Integrating innovation successfully is a common challenge for businesses, but one that many struggle to overcome.

This book provides not only an understanding of why this happens but also actionable steps to overcome it. Offering practical solutions and a fresh perspective, the book illustrates the correlation between innovation and business development and shows how they can complement each other to create a successful business strategy.

From identifying relevant problems to scouting for the right technology and building a meaningful network of partners, this book covers a wide range of topics. It is therefore ideal for a diverse range of professionals, including new entrepreneurs who want to understand how large corporations behave, novice business development, and innovation managers who want to learn best practices and effectively navigate their roles, and experienced professionals who are looking for a structured approach to incorporate innovation.

In particular, this book is ideal for executives who aspire to transform their companies into more innovative organizations but are uncertain about the most effective strategies to do so, or have encountered previous failures. Regardless of experience level, this book offers practical guidance and a fresh perspective for taking innovation to the next level and driving it to successful execution.

Keywords

innovation implementation; corporate innovation; effective business development; structured approach to business development; identifying the problem; technology scouting; building and maintaining a network; overcoming business barriers

Contents

Foreword

Foreword 1

I had the pleasure of first working with Yaron Flint when I served as CTO of Stanley Black and Decker. Visiting his homeland for the first time in 2018, I was immediately impressed by the highly collaborative, innovative, and customer-focused entrepreneurial culture of innovation. As a leader, Yaron's global network of innovators proved immediately useful; however, his experience and hard-earned wisdom offered long-term benefits. Fortunately for you, the latter is now encapsulated in this enlightening text.

This book is a distillation of Yaron's unique insight into business development, business incubation, and customer-centricity. In his text, the reader will find a goldmine of principles and best practices in business development and innovation culled from decades of explorations, failures, and successes. His business development frame of reference is particularly valuable as experienced intrapreneurs and entrepreneurs know that sales to paying customers can be more important than investment funding, because customer purchases validate needs served by transformative products or services.

The book contains value for multiple communities including inventors, entrepreneurs, investors, and leaders who are motivated to create lasting value. Unlike other books on business development, innovation is viewed through the lens of business development and the generation of a long-term value by taking a market and customer-centric approach that leverages partnerships and networks to build higher-value ecosystems. The author explains why large companies fail to innovate and provide a phased-based recipe for innovation, identifies common pitfalls, and describes methods to overcome barriers, especially challenging in enterprises.

By blending guidelines, methods, and stories, the book provides an accessible and practical set of actions of benefit to a range of readers.

The value of the text is enhanced by several key appendices. These include a guide to the most relevant chapters tailored to different audiences such as entrepreneurs, business developers, innovation managers, or executives. Another handy appendix summarizes key elements of business development foundations and how they apply to innovation exploration.

A fresh and welcome perspective on new product and service development, this book succinctly and clearly describes a structured approach to innovation employing business development best practices. The comprehensive framework will be a valuable guide to both novices and experienced business veterans who will find inspirationally concrete advice on how to create enduring value and customers who advocate for your business.

Best wishes in your business development journey!
Dr. Mark Maybury
www.linkedin.com/in/dr-mark-t-maybury-28532/

Foreword 2

After working with, and helping, literally, thousands of companies in virtually all industries and in over 75 countries become more creative, I have come to two clear insights:

1. Every company in the world wants to innovate.
2. No one seems to know how to make it happen.

Oh, do not get me wrong, there are some amazingly innovative companies out there, and more or less every single business leader will talk about the need for innovation.

But extremely few of them actually know how to do it. They do not have a system, do not understand the process, and cannot describe how they do it when they do manage to do it.

That is why this book is so important. It is a guide to how to create an organization that innovates. It is a manual for innovation success. It is a go-to resource to make sure you do not forget some important aspects of innovation.

It is the answer you have been looking for.

This book is written by one of the most passionate corporate leaders I have had the privilege to learn from in my 25+ years of interviewing thousands upon thousands of top innovation managers.

Yaron is smart, clear, structured, focused, and insightful.
And so is this book of his.
Welcome to the world of Innovative Business Development.
Prepare to learn.

—Fredrik Haren, The Creativity Explorer.

Acknowledgments

The inspiration for this book emerged from a personal pain point that I struggled with for years throughout my career; the challenge of finding a clear and practical approach to effectively incorporate innovation. Despite my desire to bring new ideas to execution, I often found myself overwhelmed by the intricacy and vagueness of the process. Through the guidance and support of numerous colleagues, friends, and companies I collaborated with, I was able to learn the ropes and develop a comprehensive understanding of the innovation incorporation process.

During the process of developing a framework and strategy to promote innovation, I realized the importance of understanding the fundamentals of how things are constructed and utilized. As a result, I wanted to share these insights with others to help them in their innovation endeavors.

I would like to express my sincere appreciation to the following people, without whom this book would not have been possible:

I am especially grateful to my wonderful wife, Shlomit, who believed in me and pushed me every step of the way. Additionally, I would like to extend my appreciation to my loving children, Alon and Noga, for being understanding and allowing me the peace and quiet to write.

I am deeply grateful to my editor, Scott Isenberg, and my collection editor, Jim Spohrer, for their insightful feedback and unwavering dedication to this project. Their expert guidance and thorough editing helped me refine my ideas and bring this book to life.

I would also like to thank my dear friends who had a tremendous contribution to this book:

To Fredrik Härén, an amazing person and a true creativity explorer who is also the most curious person I have ever met. His invaluable insights, guidance, and support have been instrumental.

To Dr. Mark Maybury, a true innovator and thought leader, for providing valuable insights and contributing to this book by writing a foreword.

To Alexander Satanowsky for sharing his experience and providing valuable insights.

To Nils Berkemeyer, the best sparring partner a person could have, who had helped me refine many of my thoughts and ideas.

To my Co-pace and SBD team members and friends for putting up with me and letting me do what I do best and to Jurgen Bilo and Eran Sandhaus who believed in me and gave me the first real chance to show what I can do.

A special thanks to my beta readers Brad Roberts, Joseph Cox, Harry Glazer, Jessica Persson, Ruti Arazi Sheffer, Mike Rolfes, Ramana Gogula, and Uri Pachter, for their thoughtful critiques and suggestions. Your feedback helped me identify areas that needed improvement and refine my message.

Finally, I would like to acknowledge the many friends and colleagues who have supported me along the way. Thank you for sharing with me your wisdom and experience. I can say that I am truly blessed to have met you all and having the chance to learn from you.

Your encouragement and enthusiasm have meant the world to me.

Thank you all from the bottom of my heart.

Introduction

Innovation is the key to success in today's ever-changing business landscape. With new technologies and market demands emerging every day, companies must be agile and forward-thinking to stay ahead of the competition and meet customer needs. This is where an innovative approach to business development comes in.

Implementing innovation requires more than just good ideas, and many companies struggle with taking their innovative ideas to the next level and turning them into reality. This book aims to provide a comprehensive framework, the tools, and strategies needed to take innovative ideas to the next level and execute them successfully.

The book will provide practical strategies for integrating innovation into businesses, following the cycle from generating ideas to executing them. It will offer insights into identifying opportunities for innovation, fostering a culture of innovation within organizations, and overcoming common obstacles that arise during the innovation integration process.

The book will also explore the field of business development and provide guidance on becoming an effective business development manager. It will highlight the importance of promoting and driving progress and introduce a structured approach to business development as a profession with its own unique features, rather than the opportunistic approach that many see it. The book will then demonstrate how innovation can be integrated into corporations by leveraging these strategies and adopting business development best practices.

Unlike many other books on innovation, sales, or business development, this book focuses on actionable items and provides a structured approach toward implementing innovation via business development. Therefore, the first few chapters cover the basics, while later chapters focus on using these fundamentals as actionable items. In the final chapters, the book provides recommendations and tips for overcoming common barriers. If you feel confident in your grasp of the basics of business development, you might want to advance to chapter 3.

However, I strongly believe that reviewing the fundamentals would still be valuable, and therefore recommend going through them as well, since they will provide some fresh insights.

Given the intention to take a more practical approach and not examine innovation and business development just from a bird's view, the book will strive to avoid an overly academic format. Instead, it will emphasize practical insights and tools that can serve as a guide for daily operations.

The idea for this book came from a true pain point, struggling to figure out the right approach to push things forward. The methodology was developed over the years learning from colleagues and through trial and error across various sectors and cultures, providing a unique insight into what works and what would be better to avoid.

The process of implementing innovation through business development can be a tedious one, but for those who are passionate about it, the rewards are well worth the effort. Although it may seem overwhelming at first, having the right tools and strategies can make the process more manageable and ultimately more fulfilling. By embracing the challenge and staying committed to the task, the journey toward successful innovation can be an incredibly satisfying one.

The book is targeted toward entrepreneurs, business leaders, and anyone interested in innovation and business development. It will appeal to individuals and organizations that want to foster innovation and turn their ideas into successful products or services within corporations.

Whether you are a novice business development manager looking to enhance your skills, an experienced one seeking to adopt a more structured approach, or an executive who believes they understand what it takes to turn innovation into success, this book will provide you with valuable insights and practical tools throughout your innovation journey.

CHAPTER 1

The Intersection of Business Development and Innovation

There are many definitions for innovation, following many books and articles that have been written on this subject, devoted to defining it and promoting its adoption.

If we want to explain what innovation is all about, I believe that the most simplistic way to describe it would be the transformation of ideas into new or improved products.

This is of course a rather wide definition that leaves much room for interpretation, but in my view, real innovation in the business world goes hand in hand with business development.

Business development, by definition, aims to seek out ideas, initiatives, and activities aimed toward value creation in the long run. This includes long-term growth in terms of business expansion, increasing profitability by building strategic partnerships, and incorporating new revenue streams and products.

Therefore, innovation would be the first stage by generating new ideas and finding ways to incorporate them, while business development should take them to the next level. It is more on how you take these ideas and concepts to the execution level within the company.

As I see it, innovation is essential for long-term sustainability and growth. Companies that fail to innovate run the risk of becoming stagnant, losing their relevance, and being overtaken by more innovative competitors, which can ultimately lead to their downfall. Innovation can also help companies adapt to changing market conditions, technological advancements, and regulatory requirements. However, and I cannot emphasize this enough, eventually, it is all about the execution; otherwise you remain in the realm of daydreaming. You could have the best ideas out there, but if you do not figure out how to take them to the next level, they will remain just great ideas.

While innovation can be an important part of business development, it is important to point out that not all innovation will necessarily lead to business development and not all business development requires innovation. Business development could also include exploring untapped customer segments for existing products or services, as well as entering new markets with established offerings.

For me, however, true innovation happens when these two interact together and where business development becomes the next natural phase of an innovative idea, looking at how to incorporate it. One of the best examples to illustrate this would be by connecting two existing solutions that did not co-exist before; instead of reinventing the wheel, you simply learn how to utilize it differently.

Bringing, for example, two sectors together like Automotive and Healthcare, Agriculture and Robotics, or even new materials to a traditional sector, could lead to new and exciting products and could help reshape the sectors you are working in.

Creating a Minimum Viable Product (MVP) of a healthcare device that monitors the driver's health while driving is an innovative idea that combines two worlds together, but finding the right partners and the right business model and working on a way to truly integrate such a product are the next phases of business development.

In summary, innovation and business development are both important aspects of business, but they involve different processes and objectives. Innovation involves creating new ideas and products, while business development involves identifying and pursuing new business opportunities to drive growth and profitability.

I will, therefore, focus on this exact process from idea to implementation, using business development processes to do so.

CHAPTER 2

The Importance of Business Development

Business development is crucial for the growth and success of any business. It involves identifying opportunities for long-term growth, creating strategies to pursue those opportunities, and implementing those strategies to achieve business goals. It requires a structured approach to analyze and understand the market you operate in, generating a deep understanding of customer needs and competitors' strategies and the ability to look beyond and identify other potential opportunities to grow your business. Therefore, I would claim that business development has mostly to do with the external world. Of course, you will need to understand what your company is doing, but you do so by looking at the market it is operating in, customers, and partnerships outside, trying to identify and find the right path for the future growth of the company.

This chapter therefore delves into the fundamentals of business development. If you feel confident in your knowledge of these basics, you may choose to skip ahead to the following chapter. However, I encourage you to read this chapter as well, as it offers fresh insights into building and maintaining a network that may prove valuable even to those who are already familiar with the fundamentals.

2.1 Corner Stones for Effective Business Development

For business development to become effective, you need to adopt long-term thinking, seek out new opportunities with current and potential future customers, as well as look into new markets while finding ways to increase your share in the market you are already operating in.

2.1.1 Generating Long-Term Value

A company can improve its margin by either increasing revenue or by reducing costs. That is as far as the basics of economics go. While reducing the costs and making the company more efficient is the work of internal processes, increasing revenue is mostly to do with the external world, by either obtaining more customers, growing sales with the ones the company already has, or finding new revenue streams altogether. Looking for these new ways to increase revenues that are not necessarily linked directly to the company's core, falls in the realm of business development and innovative thinking. There are many challenges however along this process, as I will cover later, either because the company is not "wired" to think in this way, or simply due to the fact that humans find it difficult to look for things outside of their comfort zone, let alone pursue them.

I. Opportunity—New Revenue Stream/New Profit Center

Finding new revenue streams is always quite challenging. It is not easy to convince people to step out of their comfort zone and what they know, especially when it is in a traditional company that has been operating in the same way for decades. However, sometimes this is the right move, either because the current market that the company is operating in has become saturated, or simply because the company has exploited all growth opportunities available.

Finding a new revenue stream or profit center can be achieved by introducing new products or services, leveraging existing assets and capabilities, or expanding into new markets, as I will cover later.

Introducing New Products or Services.   When talking about new products or services, there is a defined structure and understanding for the product development process that involves ideation, design, development, testing, and launch of the new product or service in the market. The process can vary depending on the type of product, industry, and company, but generally, it follows these stages:

1. **Ideation**—The generation and evaluation of ideas for a new product or service. It includes market research, brainstorming, and idea screening.

2. **Concept development**—In this stage, the most promising ideas are refined and developed into a concept. It includes creating product specifications, defining target markets, and evaluating the feasibility of the concept.

3. **Design and prototyping**—The creation of detailed designs and the development of prototypes of the product. It includes designing of the product's appearance, functionality, and user experience.

4. **Testing and validation**—Testing and validating the product to ensure that it meets the customer's needs and expectations.

5. **Launching**—Once the product is fully developed and tested, it is launched in the market. It includes creating marketing campaigns, setting up distribution channels, and making the necessary preparations to provide assistance and address customer needs.

There could be a stage of postlaunch as well, where the new product's performance is monitored, making necessary improvements based on customer feedback.

Naturally, the product development process could be iterative, meaning that the process can be repeated multiple times until the product is perfected.

Leveraging Existing Assets and Capabilities.   For a traditional company or even individuals, it is extremely important to understand what is their unique competitive advantage, making sure this is utilized in the best way possible. For example, if a well-known high-quality parts manufacturer for the automotive world has been recently feeling that its market is becoming overcrowded or less sensitive to high-end products, it might consider moving into another sector like aviation, where its advantage is still sought after. The same goes for software engineers, cybersecurity, and Artificial Intelligence (AI) experts, leveraging their know-how to other markets.

Leveraging existing assets and capabilities therefore involves identifying and maximizing the value of resources and skills that a business already possesses. It consists of assessing their value, devising a plan to utilize them effectively, allocating resources, selecting a team to oversee the initiative, and finally, executing the plan and monitoring its progress. By taking these steps, companies can unlock the full potential of their existing assets and capabilities and achieve greater success in the market.

Overall, creating a new revenue stream or profit center requires strategic planning, allocation of resources, and effective execution. By diversifying its revenue streams, a company can increase its profitability and reduce its reliance on its core business.

II. Reducing Costs—Operations Management and Optimization

Reducing costs is another way to optimize your operations and could include the following:

- **Performance measurement**—Measuring and analyzing business performance to identify areas for improvement.
- **Process improvement**—Identifying inefficiencies in business processes and improving them to increase productivity.
- **Supply chain management**—Managing and optimizing the distribution of products from suppliers all the way to customers to ensure that products and services are delivered on time while minimizing costs.
- **Inventory management**—Managing and optimizing inventory levels to ensure that there is enough stock to meet demand while minimizing the amount of capital tied up in inventory.
- **Quality control**—Ensuring that products and services meet customer expectations and quality standards, to avoid returns and recalls.
- **Capacity planning**—Optimizing the flow of necessary resources, including materials, equipment, and personnel to address demand.
- **Project management**—Planning, monitoring, and executing projects to ensure that they are completed on time, and within budget, while maintaining high-quality standards.
- **Risk management**—The company should identify and assess the risks associated with each project and develop strategies to mitigate those risks. This may involve setting clear goals and timelines, allocating resources effectively, and conducting thorough research and testing. Additionally, the company

should be prepared with a contingency plan, if necessary, in response to changing circumstances or unexpected outcomes.

- **Information technology**—Leveraging technology to improve operational efficiency and optimize business processes. The first step is data visualization, making sure the performance is visually available across the operation and in the more advanced stage, data analytics; taking all data and analyzing it to deliver actionable items.

III. Corporate Social Responsibility

Over the last decades, corporate social responsibility has become a key factor for a company's future success and growth, due to an increase in environmental and social awareness. Today, a company needs to reflect on how to become greener and improve its impact on the environment if it wants to survive. In many cases, this means a totally different approach or delivering new and less polluting products, which could have a deep impact on the company's future plans and strategy. This push comes from the increasing expectations of various stakeholders, including customers, employees, investors, and various communities, as well as regulatory requirements.

These changes could include the following:

- **Environmental sustainability**—Implementing environmentally friendly practices to reduce the impact of business operations on the environment, such as reducing waste, conserving energy, and using renewable resources.
- **Social sustainability**—Ensuring that business operations are socially responsible and benefit the communities in which they operate, such as through fair labor practices, community engagement, and donations to charitable causes.
- **Economic sustainability**—Ensuring that business operations are economically sustainable and contribute to long-term growth and profitability, while creating value for stakeholders, such as circular economy and recycling.

- **Ethical business practices**—Conducting business in an ethical and transparent way, including complying with laws and regulations, avoiding conflicts of interest, and protecting the privacy and confidentiality of various stakeholders. The issue of data privacy, for example, has generated a huge impact on how companies absorb and utilize data and how they could engage with their customers.
- **Reporting and transparency**—Reporting on sustainability and Corporate Social Responsibility performance to stakeholders, including sustainability reports and other communications.
- **Supply chain management**—Ensuring that suppliers and partners also follow sustainable and socially responsible practices, including responsible sourcing and supplier audits.

One of the biggest challenges in incorporating environmentally friendly solutions is the perceived lack of Return on Investment (ROI). Many companies are hesitant to invest in environmentally friendly practices or technologies because they do not see an immediate or significant financial benefit. As a result, you can witness many companies that are simply focused on carbon offsets and credits rather than truly implementing a greener solution.

Therefore, there is a significant push to identify green solutions that would not cause an increase in expenses and even reduce them.

There are several arguments for why incorporating environmental solutions can actually lead to long-term financial benefits. For example:

- **Cost savings**—Implementing energy-efficient practices or switching to renewable energy sources could potentially lead to significant cost savings in the long run by reducing energy bills. For instance, carbon utilization involves capturing CO_2 emissions and converting them into useful products like fuels, chemicals, and building materials. Another example is the reuse of steam generated in power plants to generate heat for industrial processes or heating of buildings.

- **Increasing durability**—Identifying eco-friendly materials that offer enhanced performance. For example, innovative polymers and composite materials have emerged as potential substitutes for metallic components, while biodegradable bioplastics have shown promise in replacing conventional trimmer lines used in grass trimmers.
- **Increased customer loyalty**—As discussed, many consumers are increasingly choosing to do business with companies that prioritize sustainability. For example, the use of biodegradable solutions is a sustainable practice that can attract customers who prioritize eco-friendliness.
- **Regulatory compliance**—Many countries and regions are implementing regulations and incentives to encourage environmental sustainability. Incorporating environmental solutions can help companies stay compliant and take advantage of these incentives. For example, water treatment solutions for factories or circular economy practices.

Overall, while there may be short-term expenditures associated with incorporating environmental solutions, the long-term benefits can outweigh these costs and lead to increased financial stability and success. As sustainability continues to gain momentum and businesses increasingly prioritize responsible practices, we can anticipate a rise in innovative solutions that balance environmental impact with economic feasibility. As companies begin to understand the long-term advantages of eco-friendly practices, we can expect to see a wider adoption of sustainable solutions across different industries.

2.1.2 Customer Relationship

Customer relationship is a critical factor for business development. Building strong and lasting relationships with customers is essential for the growth and success of any business. Locating the right customers, expanding the customer base, and maintaining their loyalty would make the entire difference between being able to grow as a business and increasing revenues or losing market share to competitors.

I. Customer Discovery

Over the past few decades, customers have become increasingly demanding in their expectations of products and services. With the rise of digital technology and the Internet, customers now have access to a wealth of information and options. This has led to a shift in power from the companies to customers, as they are now able to quickly compare and choose between different products and services.

In today's market, consumers demand more than just high-quality products and services. They desire a personalized experience that caters to their unique and changing needs and preferences, while still providing exceptional customer service. In addition, customers are becoming more socially conscious, and are looking to conduct business only with those companies who comply with their set of values.

This shift in customer expectations has forced companies to adapt and innovate in order to stay competitive. Those that fail to meet customer demands, risk losing market share and relevance in today's fast-paced business environment. As a result, companies are now investing heavily in understanding and addressing customer needs and are constantly searching for new ways to differentiate themselves and stand out from the competition.

Large and stable companies have become less appealing compared to the past and customers feel more and more comfortable engaging directly with startups, specifically around software-related services, which feature less stickiness than traditional hardware solutions. The personal touch and personalization are very challenging to experience from a large corporation, and therefore, customers have less of a problem shifting from one company to the other.

Finding a customer that is willing to explore new opportunities has become easier, but on the flip side, these customers have less patience and would move away if their expectations are not met fast enough. Therefore, finding the right balance between exploring new opportunities while still remaining in focus, has become more and more challenging.

One way to keep this balance is by getting to know your customers better. It is not at all about what your customer thinks and feels about your relationship and products, but rather what are the customer's needs and pain points that you could address. Doing so requires abandoning all preconceptions you might have and focusing on the objective truth, as I will cover later.

II. Customer Acquisition and Retention

Customer acquisition and retention are two critical components of any successful business strategy. Customer acquisition refers to the process of attracting new customers to a business, while customer retention is focused on keeping existing customers satisfied and loyal over the long term.

Acquiring new customers could be a costly and rather time-consuming process, which is why it is important for companies to have a targeted and effective approach. This may include strategies such as content marketing, targeted advertising, and referral programs to encourage existing customers to remain loyal.

However, customer acquisition is only part of the equation. Retaining existing customers is equally important, as it costs much less to retain a customer than it does to acquire a new one. To retain customers, companies must focus on providing excellent customer service, building strong relationships and a customer interface, and continually improving their products and services to meet customers' expectations and changing needs. In the dynamic business environment of today, many customers prefer companies that offer a superior customer interface and personalized products over those that focus solely on outperforming technical capabilities.

In today's digital age, social media and online reviews have also become important factors in customer acquisition and retention. Companies that had no idea of how to approach this world before, must learn how to actively manage their online branding and engage with customers through social media channels in addition, to build trust and loyalty.

2.1.3 Market Opportunities

Knowing your market well is critical for the long-term success of any business. By understanding your customers and competitors, you can make informed decisions that drive growth and profitability.

By knowing your market well, you can tailor your products and services to meet the needs of your customers without addressing each one individually. This can help you build a loyal customer base and differentiate your company from competitors although producing more generic solutions, yet still providing the feeling of a personal touch. Additionally, understanding the competitive landscape can help you identify potential threats and opportunities, and make informed decisions about pricing, marketing, and product development.

During my past experience as an investor, one of the most critical factors in deciding whether to invest in a company was how well they knew the market they were operating in. Understanding the market goes beyond knowing the obvious competitors; it involves identifying future threats and understanding the company's position within the market.

A company that lacks a deep understanding of their market is unlikely to survive in the long run. They will be caught off guard by unexpected challenges and may not have the necessary strategies in place to address them effectively.

In today's fast-paced business world, keeping up with the changes in the market is essential. The market is constantly evolving, and companies that do not stay up-to-date risk losing their competitive edge. This involves continuously monitoring the market, identifying emerging trends, and adjusting strategy accordingly. Companies may need to pivot their business model, develop new products or services, or enter new markets to stay ahead of the competition.

It is more than just keeping a close eye on the new trends and what is the competition doing. It is important to learn about new technologies from other sectors that could become a potential threat to the market you are operating in, and Blockbuster is a great example of not paying such attention by perceiving live streaming as a threat in time. The story goes that Marc Randolph, the co-founder of Netflix, tried to sell Netflix to Blockbuster at one point for $50 million but was "laughed out of the room"—a $150 billion mistake.

One of the key techniques to know your market well and to evaluate new potential markets is by conducting thorough market research and analysis and making sure that they are always kept up to date.

I. Market Research and Analysis

Market research is the base for understanding the market and is done through the process of gathering and analyzing information about the particular market or industry in question. It is a critical foundation for any successful business strategy, as it provides valuable insights into current and potential customer needs, preferences, and behaviors.

Market research can be used to identify new growth opportunities, understand market trends and competitive dynamics, and make informed decisions about product development, pricing, and marketing. It typically involves a combination of quantitative and qualitative research methods, such as surveys, focus groups, and data analysis.

The benefits of market research are numerous. By conducting research, companies can better understand their customers and tailor their products and services to meet their needs. They can also identify new customer segments and develop targeted marketing campaigns to reach them. Additionally, market research can help companies stay ahead of competitors by identifying emerging trends and potential threats to their market position.

However, market research can also be costly and time-consuming, which is why it is important for companies to carefully consider their research objectives and methodology before embarking on a research project. It is also important to ensure that research findings are properly interpreted and used to make informed business decisions.

There is no value in performing the best analysis possible just to find it sit eventually on a shelf in some executive's room.

II. Competitive Analysis and Market Positioning

Competitive analysis involves identifying and analyzing your competitors, while market positioning involves defining how your business fits within the competitive landscape.

There are various tools and analytical frameworks available in the market to help organizations gain a better understanding of their market position and competition, such as a competitor analysis, a Strengths,

Weaknesses, Opportunities and Threats (SWOT) analysis, or a Porter's Five Forces analysis*.

To truly understand your competitive landscape, you must first identify who these competitors are. This may include direct competitors who offer similar products or services, as well as indirect competitors who offer alternative solutions to the same problem.

Once competitors have been identified, companies can analyze their position via a SWOT analysis, for example, to identify the company's strengths, weaknesses, opportunities, and threats in the market.

It is also important to understand various business models and pricing strategies, marketing tactics, and potential customer base. This information can be used to identify areas where the business can differentiate itself and gain a competitive advantage. It may also offer insights into the value of services you provide for free and the willingness of people to pay for them.

While conducting a competitive analysis, it is important not to fall into the same mistake many companies make; instead of trying to understand what the competitor is doing and why, they tend to focus on the features, comparing both products. Although comparing features is important to understand how your product differs from the competition, it will never provide you with a clear understanding of "why." It is therefore important to first understand where your competitors are heading, why are they doing what they are doing and what is their strategy behind. Then when you conduct a feature comparison, you can truly understand what is behind them. The distinction between being a sluggish follower, constantly playing catch-up with competitors, and being positioned to become a leader, lies in your ability to truly understand your competitors' plans and position your business accordingly.

The proper way to establish your market position is therefore by analyzing the competitive landscape and determining where your business stands. This involves identifying the unique value proposition that sets your business apart from the competition, which can only be achieved by first understanding their strategy.

It is similar to conducting military intelligence during a battle; you monitor your opponent's actions on multiple fronts, try to understand

---

* Porter, M.E. March–April, 1979. "How Competitive Forces Shape Strategy," *Harvard Business Review* 57, no. 2, pp. 137–145.

their strategy and motivations behind them, and then use that under-standing to your advantage.

Overall, competitive analysis and market positioning are essential components of any successful business strategy. By understanding the competition and defining your unique value proposition, companies can differentiate themselves and gain a competitive advantage, as well as utilize their advantages to diversify into other markets.

2.1.4 Partnerships and Collaborations

Developing new relationships and fortifying the ones you have are a very important practice in business development. Large corporations usually tend to dwell between two types of partners: suppliers or customers. Being able to identify those partners who do not necessarily fall under these categories is challenging and requires an open-minded approach and forthcoming vision. However, forming strategic alliances with these partners could provide access to new markets, technologies, or resources.

By working together with other organizations, the company can access new ideas and perspectives, combine resources and expertise, and create synergies that can enhance current operations. These partnerships can take various forms, such as joint ventures, research and development agreements, or strategic alliances.

One important aspect of relationships that is not addressed as much as it should is the issue of relationship maintenance. There is a tendency to overlook this, but business relationships are the same as day-to-day ones and keeping and maintaining these relationships are crucial for both day-to-day operations and future exploration.

2.2 Business Development Versus Sales

In more than a few companies I came across over the years, I have noticed a tendency to confuse business development and sales.

In my experience, the two are certainly linked together but are not the same and obviously cannot be run by the same person.

Sales focus is, by definition, mostly short-term thinking, or how to grow your top line during a given period. A good salesperson would push to close a deal and would most certainly understand the delicate balance between incentives and growing revenue. Sales managers are usually compensated by achieving sales goals, so they would do whatever is in their power to push for a sale, sometimes even at the expense of long-term relationships.

Business development, on the other hand, is more long-term thinking, looking for new growth fields and new opportunities and building up relationships over time.

The best synergy between sales and business development is for the business development side to build up the relationships with potential customers and look for additional revenue streams and once these materialize, to hand them over to the sales side to be executed.

Confusing the two is basically confusing tactics with strategy, and unfortunately, many companies tend to do so and might put the wrong person in place. The different focus requires a different skill set and even an exceptional person in one field does not necessarily mean he will do well in the other.

2.3 Unique Qualifications for a Business Development Manager

By now, you should have a clear understanding of why business development should be treated as a profession by itself, rather than simply an opportunistic change from another position. A successful business development manager should be an innovative, out-of-box thinker, while being able to challenge the current conceptions. The manager needs to be able to both invigorate and spur to action external partners as well as the managers internally while keeping a positive thinking and pushing forward.

These qualifications could be taught of course but need to develop over time to achieve the best outcome. In the same way, you can teach a physician his practice, but the best ones require the time and experience to reach the level of knowledge and expertise to become truly valuable.

Hence, exceptional business development managers are not easy to find, as they necessitate a distinctive skill set and relevant experience that include:

1. **Storytelling**

   Whenever people inquire about how I managed to drive projects forward throughout my career and what was my greatest asset in doing so, my answer is always the same: "I am a very good story-teller." Eventually having the vision is not enough and in order to push something that you truly believe in, you need to be able to bring people along to the ride, while some of them do not want to participate at all. Therefore, being able to understand what that person is passionate about and spin it in a way that he would want to get on board, is very much like storytelling; understanding your audience and spinning the tale in a way that they will relate to and would want to participate in. For example, if you want to push for a new invisible marker in tires, for some people the story would be sustainability and circular economy, for others it would be around the technology or just being first to market with such a technology.

2. **Network as a key**
   The biggest assets of a business development manager are the relationships and reputation he has. Being able to hop on a phone call and drive people to action, or just get some input that is needed, is an asset that some companies would be willing to pay dearly for. Therefore, maintaining these relationships and good reputation are the assets you need to cherish most and never do anything that could jeopardize them. External companies need to know that they can trust you to keep their best interests at heart. Therefore, if you observe any misuse of power by the organization over a startup, it is important, and moreover, your duty, to take a firm stand and protect not just the startup but also the corporate's brand and reputation from any potential damage caused by employees who may not fully comprehend the consequences of their actions.

3. **Passion and energy**
   There is no bigger turnoff than hearing someone speak in a dull way on a product or new opportunity. Of course, you should not get too excited, but if the person across you does not believe that you are truly passionate about the topic you are presenting, he will not be convinced. After all, how can you convince others if you are not convinced (and show it) yourself?

4. Creative—Thinking outside the box

A good business development manager needs to be able to look at different paths and envision how they interact together in a way that others might not see. It does not mean that he needs to be a deep technical expert; for that you have internal teams and experts to evaluate ideas but rather have a very good understanding of many topics so he could follow the connection points and envision how they could interact. The worst thing for a business development manager is to be an expert in one topic. This will most likely move him from business development to the product enhancement realm.

5. People's person

Since it is important to get as many people on board as possible, an effective business development manager should possess strong interpersonal skills and the ability to communicate effectively with individuals from diverse backgrounds and levels of seniority. In addition, the manager needs to know how to interact with stakeholders both externally, such as accelerators, Venture Capitals (VCs), scouts, and other companies' representatives, and internally like the product team, engineers, legal, and finance, and talk to them in their unique way and style so they would relate to him. Not challenging these stakeholders while sometimes navigating them in another direction is an art by itself and requires the ability to put your ego aside, while still providing the other side with a sense of value, so they will want to continue working with you.

Knowing when to push something and how to do so in the right and most effective way is key and therefore business development managers need to have high emotional intelligence and be tuned to the other side and what is going on.

6. Ability to analyze complex environments

In a large corporation, identifying the key individuals who can drive progress and facilitate decision making is crucial for achieving goals and making meaningful change. Most times it will not necessarily be the top executives, but rather regular employees that everyone looks up to and listens to what they have to say.

A great way to identify key personnel is to conduct multiple interviews with various employees and ask them for recommendations for individuals who can drive progress in their division. The names that keep resurfacing are the ones you want to target and get to know better.

7. Long-term vision and execution

Short-term thinking does not belong to the business development realm and is mostly in the area of sales.

While having a long-term vision is important, it is not enough to ensure success. It is equally essential to be able to translate that vision into actionable steps that can be implemented. A great exercise would be to create a written plan that outlines each step required to achieve the end goal. This plan should be comprehensive and include a business case that clearly articulates the benefits and feasibility of the proposed approach. Additionally, it is essential to identify and engage the right people who can contribute to the success of the plan. The more specific you get, the more you will understand what is yet to be done.

However, it is important to maintain a degree of flexibility when planning for the future, as unforeseen circumstances and changing market conditions can impact even the most well-crafted plans. Remember that good plans are always a good foundation for change and even God had only a seven-day plan.

8. Gut feeling

A skilled business development manager possesses a unique ability to identify potential connections and opportunities that others may overlook. They may have a strong conviction that certain topics or ideas need to be promoted within the organization, even in the face of initial skepticism or resistance. People who do not relate to this might dismiss it as no more than "gut feeling," but as a business development manager gains experience, their success increasingly becomes a function of both their expertise and practical know-how. To continue the physician analogy, this is similar to an experienced physician who can quickly diagnose a patient's condition based on a brief examination. This is not merely a matter of intuition, but rather a function of their experience with similar cases and their ability to draw insights from them.

This skill set could be very important to reduce risk and move fast, although some organizations might not feel the same. It is similar to a gunman in the far west who shoots fast without aiming, considering all his years of practice, compared to someone who takes the time to analyze the wind influence and trajectory without ever taking the shot. It is about minimizing the risk while taking a chance, rather than avoiding it altogether.

It is important to understand however that this could not be a replacement to a proper analysis, but rather an enhancement to it, where the analysis comes in addition for validation, in the same way that the above physician would call for tests to validate his hypothesis.

2.4 Building and Maintaining a Network

Building a network is important for personal and professional development. It provides access to new opportunities, knowledge sharing, support, collaboration, reputation building, and diversity. Building a strong and diverse network can help individuals and companies achieve their goals and reach their full potential. Therefore, it is not surprising that it is by far one of the strongest assets a good business development manager should have. The better and more experienced the manager is, the more comprehensive and sizable his network should be. This allows the manager to identify new and innovative technologies, and to quickly gain an understanding of their potential value and impact while bypassing the competition. A good business development or innovation manager cannot know everything, so knowing the right amount of people who could collectively cover everything is the next best thing.

However, the bigger the network is, the harder and more challenging it becomes to maintain and control it, and therefore, given the importance of the topic, I thought it could be helpful to add some pointers on how to build and maintain a proper network.

This could be relevant for those seeking to move to another sector they have no connections to, or just establish a local network in a new location.

2.4.1 *Building a Network*

Throughout my career, I found myself in markets where I had no prior knowledge or connections and had to quickly figure out how to navigate my way. One memorable example was from early in my career when I was evaluating a deal in India and was unexpectedly presented with another deal that seemed much more promising. The only problem was that this deal was located four hours away in an area where I had no connections or prior knowledge.

To overcome this challenge, I knew that I had to leverage my network and find the right connections to succeed. Fortunately, my prior work experience had prepared me well for this challenge. Having worked for one of the top accounting firms in the world, I had spent some time building a strong network of industry contacts and partners.

With this in mind, I reached out to a partner whom I knew well, and he was able to connect me with his Indian counterpart. This individual proved to be an invaluable resource in navigating the local market and making meaningful connections.

This experience taught me the importance of networking and building strong relationships. As a business development manager, the ability to create and maintain meaningful connections can make all the difference in achieving success in new markets and unfamiliar territories.

In my opinion, an effective business development manager primarily operates based on their extensive experience and knowledge of what works best. This involves analyzing successful and unsuccessful approaches over the years. While it was difficult to condense this knowledge into a list, I have come up with several key areas that I have found to be helpful in building a valuable network.

1. **Identifying and creating a personal relationship with community leaders**

   The first thing is to get yourself known in the market you would like to operate in, and the best way to do so is by getting introduced to those who are considered community leaders or influencers. Identifying these individuals is quite simple, very similar to identifying them in your organization, just ask who are the ones you should meet and the names that keep surfacing are the ones you should target. Try to get to them by a warm introduction from your current network of people you know well, since this will already put you in a better position once you meet.

2. Spend Time With Startups

Startups are the backbone of any sector you operate in and therefore getting to know them will carry your name out there, especially if you spend time with them and bring them value. There are connections among entrepreneurs who know each other from past experience, and they tend to share insights, so if you spend time with a few of them and provide them value, your name will get out there.

3. Be Accessible

People need to know that they can reach you and get to meet you, otherwise you will not be recommended as a key person to know. Make sure you dedicate time to talk to people and meet them in person. To be clear, this is not something you should expect to be compensated for and is rather an investment in your future.

4. Leveraging Key Stakeholders

Leverage key stakeholders working with startups for deal flow and connections. This does not apply only to investors like VCs or angels but also to service providers like law firms and accountants. Every startup needs these services too and most of these firms have designated departments to deal with startups. Since these firms try to provide additional value to their customers, getting to know them and making yourself accessible, is just a win-win situation to enlarge deal flow and promote your reputation.

5. Work on Many Small Wins

Securing a significant deal can undoubtedly enhance your reputation and attract more people who would like to meet you, but it necessitates a substantial investment of time and effort. Ultimately, your success depends on building relationships and increasing your visibility, which requires consistent effort. As such, even minor actions such as introducing startups to your network can be as valuable as closing a significant deal or investment. Therefore, it is essential to work on both big and small opportunities to maximize your impact and reputation.

6. **Participate in Key Events**

People need to see you and feel that you are a crucial part of the ecosystem. Make sure to choose these events wisely; the ones with high exposure have the tendency to be too big to be able to meet all the relevant people and you simply cannot participate in all the small ones. A good balance between the two is always a good idea.

Strive to take part in panels and keynote speaking; apart from being able to share your knowledge and experience, it is much more efficient to have people come to you because they heard you, rather than trying to reach people one by one.

7. **Never Say No to an Interesting Meeting**

Expanding your network over time is critical to your success, and it requires a proactive approach to meeting new people, not just those in your industry. Building relationships with individuals in other sectors can be just as valuable, if not more so, in growing and diversifying your network over time. In fact, connecting with experts from other domains can help you strengthen your network by bringing in fresh perspectives and ideas. Therefore, it is crucial to actively seek out new connections and make an effort to build relationships with individuals outside of your current network.

8. **Make It Personal**

Making a personal connection is key to leaving a lasting impression on someone. When meeting new people, it is important to keep things informal and avoid delving into business matters right away. Instead, focus on building a relationship and getting to know the individual on a personal level. Therefore, try to avoid addressing business during first encounters, for that you could have a separate and dedicated follow-up meeting.

2.4.2 Maintaining a Network

The ability to build a meaningful network is just the first step since it would be totally useless if you are not able to maintain it. Many people fail to understand that maintaining a meaningful network is almost a full-time job, so knowing what to do could truly help and would allow you to keep on building and enlarging your network as you go.

Through my professional experience, I have found the following key elements to be beneficial in cultivating and strengthening your network:

1. **Strive to Make Cross Connections Within Your Network**
   The best way to create immediate value within your network is by constantly trying to make connections between different people across your network. These should be very precise and pinpointed, otherwise people will stop following your introductions and see this as a nuisance. When connecting two people in your network, specifically if it goes well, both parties will hold you in high esteem and feel that a connection to you has benefited them and therefore would want to keep in touch.

2. **Bring Value to the Eco-system You Are Part of**
   If you are part of a specific ecosystem, strive to bring value to the ecosystem in general. Help companies and take an active part in main events, so people would seek out your kinship. If you are not part of any ecosystem, well, then you are not a very good business development manager.

3. **Strive to Provide Value in Every Meeting**
   People tend to maintain contact with individuals they believe have brought value to them in some way and distance themselves from those they perceive as "takers." It is therefore very important to never step out of a meeting without feeling that you brought value to the other side.

   Leave some time at the end of a meeting to ask the question of "How can I help you?" even if that was not the intention of the meeting.

4. **Establish a Foundation Before Attempting to Sell**

   Many people feel that they might have a one-shot chance and there-fore try to condense as much as possible into a meeting, turning it into a sales pitch, failing to understand that this is simply a turnoff. People dislike it when others try to impose something on them in an initial meeting. Treat this as if you were courting someone rather than being at a pickup bar. The intention is to generate enough curi-osity to turn this into a follow-up meeting where you can get to know the person better. Remember that you are building a relation-ship rather than trying to close an immediate deal.

5. **Remembering the Small Things**

   Having a good memory is always a plus, but you could use cheat cards or notes to write important and interesting facts about the person you met. Go over them before your next meeting and this way, the next time you meet will feel more personal.

6. **Meeting and Socializing**

   Participating in events is not just about expanding your network, it is also about maintaining it and fostering long-term relationships. By actively engaging and showing your commitment to the ecosys-tem, you increase the likelihood of being viewed as an important member of the community. On the other hand, if you do not attend events, others may perceive you as disinterested in maintaining rela-tionships and overlook you as a valuable member of their network. Treat events the same way you would treat a business meeting and spend enough time with everyone that could be of importance to you. You can have follow-up meetings for lunch or coffee with those you feel closer to and give them your undivided attention, but events should be utilized to be seen and increase your exposure. The way I see it, a person would appreciate a five-minute talk to you during an event, when he sees how busy you are, more than if you spent thirty minutes or one hour with him during that event. Again, there are always follow-ups, and it is important to set some time aside for those too.

7. **Utilize the Social Media**

Various platforms like Facebook and particularly LinkedIn provide an excellent means of keeping tabs on the people in your network; you can peruse their latest publications, track their job changes, or acknowledge personal milestones such as birthdays. It is imperative to dedicate some time to these social media channels and engage with the people in your network. This will help you stay connected while staying up to date with the latest developments. Ensure that you keep your network abreast of any significant developments in your professional or personal life and allocate some time to produce and publish professional content.

8. **"Mouth to ear" Is Slow but Efficient**

Your goal would be eventually to have people talk highly of you behind your back. If someone hears good things about you from multiple sources, he would like to meet you and spend time with you, so make sure you leave a good impression wherever you go.

As mentioned, external stakeholders need to know that they can trust you to keep their best interests in mind. So be open and frank as much as you can, do not ruin future relationships for a short-term achievement, and remember, your network and reputation are the biggest assets you have as a business development manager that follow you wherever you go.

CHAPTER 3

A Company's Journey Toward Innovation

In these ever-changing times with dire business headwinds, how companies quickly innovate could be their lifeline into the future. Whenever a company decides to go down the path of trying to become more innovative, there is almost always the debate of Internal versus External. In other words, could the company do it all in-house with its own resources, or should it go external and collaborate with another company.

Going external does not always simplify the process and minimize disagreements. There is often a conflict between the right approach, whether it involves buying, investing, or partnering for mutual benefit.

Further in the book, I will explore different approaches to onboarding innovation and examine the reasons why some companies thrive while others struggle on their innovation journey.

3.1 Experience and Willingness to Adopt New Technology

Over the past few decades, there has been a significant shift in the way products are designed and developed. With the rapid advancement of technology and the increasing demand for smarter and more efficient products, the focus has shifted from hardware-driven solutions to software-driven solutions, and consequently, traditional companies have been finding it harder and harder to keep up.

One of the key drivers for this shift is the increasing complexity of products. As products become more sophisticated and interconnected, they require more advanced software to manage and control their various components and functions. For example, vehicles these days feature sophisticated electronics and software systems that control everything from the engine to the entertainment system and have basically turned the vehicle into a sophisticated computer on wheels. Even before achieving full autonomy, vehicles already contain more lines of code than a Boeing 777 or a space shuttle.

This transition is surfacing in other sectors as well, such as manufacturing, construction, and agriculture, to name a few.

Another factor driving the shift toward software-driven solutions is the increasing demand for personalization and customization. With the rise of the Internet and connected devices, consumers are now expecting products that can adapt to their individual needs and preferences. This requires products to have more advanced software capabilities that can be easily customized and updated.

One of the key benefits of connected products is the ability to collect and analyze data on their usage and performance. By gathering data on how products are being used, manufacturers can gain insights into how to improve their design and functionality, as well as identify potential issues before they become major problems.

Connected products can also enable advanced data analytics that could turn into new revenue streams and new services such as predictive maintenance, which involves the usage of data analytics and machine learning algorithms to predict when a product is likely to fail to proactively perform maintenance or repairs. This can help to reduce downtime, minimize repair costs, and extend the lifespan of the product.

Overall, the trend toward software-driven solutions is likely to continue as companies seek to create products that are more intelligent, flexible, and user-friendly, while exploring new revenue opportunities. While hardware will always remain a key component of many products, software has become increasingly critical in enabling new levels of functionality and performance.

This creates of course the need for new and skilled employees and business models that traditional companies find hard to compete with. Original Equipment Manufacturers (OEMs) hire more and more software engineers and Artificial Intelligence (AI) experts and continue to seek new business models to enable their quest for increasing traditional revenue streams.

Companies, therefore, can no longer rely on internal know-how alone and are actively seeking new technologies to learn from and incorporate into their product roadmap.

3.2 Leveraging Technology and Digital Transformation

Leveraging technology and digital transformation is essential for innovation in today's business environment. Digital transformation has the potential to transform the way companies operate, interact with customers, and create value.

Digital transformation involves the integration of digital technologies into all aspects of the business, including operations, customer experience, and product development. This may involve implementing new technologies, such as Artificial Intelligence (AI), the Internet of Things (IoT), and cloud computing, to improve processes and create new opportunities. It may also involve adopting new business models, such as subscription-based services or digital platforms, to better meet customer needs and preferences.

To leverage technology and digital transformation in a proper manner, the company should develop a relevant strategy that aligns with its overall goals and objectives. In many cases, this would be a totally new field for it and therefore will be hard to fully comprehend. A traditional company will most likely consider digital solutions as an enabler to sell more of its current products rather than a product by itself. Companies might offer a product connectivity, performance analytics, and predictive maintenance as free-of-charge services that come alongside with the product they are selling, failing to understand that these are products by themselves that customers would be willing to pay for.

By this they will most likely not allocate the right resources and investments, such as talent, infrastructure, and technology, to support the digital transformation process.

Digital transformation has become a necessity for companies to remain competitive and failing to embrace it can result in losing market share to competitors who have adopted it. Therefore, companies should view digital transformation not only as a way to sell more of their products but also as a way to prevent losing market share to competition and stay relevant in the digital age.

3.3 Innovation as Public Relations

Many companies take pride of their innovation approaches, claiming that they are ever-evolving and developing new and exciting technologies, either because they truly believe that this is their only way to move forward and be successful in this new world, or simply because their clients demand so and their competitors are pressuring them to do so.

Unfortunately, there are still many companies that have not fully grasped the potential of incorporating new external technologies, believing that they could survive merely on their brand's reputation, or keep on doing the exact same thing they have been doing for centuries. In some cases, this might be true, but in many other cases, companies do not really comprehend these trends and how the world is evolving.

Technological graveyards are filled with companies that failed to fully comprehend this, and names such as Kodak and Blockbuster serve as sobering reminders of the consequences of not doing so.

Almost every company is taking pride of being innovative, but those who have not fully grasped the potential of introducing external know-how, are doing what I like to refer to as "innovation as PR," utilizing innovation as a public relations tool rather than a genuine attempt to create new, valuable products or services. These companies may attempt to convince the outside world of their innovation capabilities but lack a true understanding of the potential and how to integrate it. For these companies, this book may not be a useful resource at this stage since they cannot fully appreciate or understand how to utilize new technologies effectively. It may be more beneficial for them to wait until they are genuinely committed to taking this path seriously.

It is relatively easy to identify such companies by examining the resources and manpower that they devote to pursuing new technologies. If a company has a limited number of personnel and no budget for innovation, it suggests that their focus is on innovation as a PR rather than a strategic objective.

On the other hand, companies that prioritize innovation and dedicate significant attention and resources to it are the ones that are more likely to benefit from this book. It can help them identify the most effective route to innovation, remain focused on their objectives, and achieve their goals more efficiently.

It is worth highlighting however that an over-indexed company is not ideal too, and certain organizations may go too far in the opposite direction by having an excessive number of internal teams focused on innovation. Therefore, establishing clear boundaries and expectations, alongside the innovation strategy, is essential to avoid such situations.

3.4 The Road Toward Innovation

Companies that go down the path toward innovation tend to follow the same pattern.

It usually starts with a self-development phase, trying to develop everything **inhouse.**

Then, as products become more complex and fragmentized and the company understands they cannot do everything by themselves, they move on to the **external know-how exploration.**

In this exploration phase, most companies tend to struggle with what would be the right framework and approach toward external collaboration. While experimenting, they mature and understand what would be the best way to onboard these new and exciting technologies they come across.

This maturity evolution can be outlined as follows:

1. **Merges and Acquisitions (M&A)**—Although the company has understood the need for external knowhow, they tend to go down the most obvious route, which is buying a company or technology and fully owning it, still not being able to disconnect themselves from the need to control everything in-house.

2. **Invest**—Once the company understands that in order to have a good stake in the game, they do not need to buy the whole external company, but rather have a foot in the door. It is also very challenging to incorporate an external company, specifically startups, into

a large organization and you might end up destroying the startup altogether when you bring it under the corporate wings.

3. **Assessment**—The corporation finds itself with an investment portfolio, trying to figure out how to generate value for the companies it already invested in.

4. **Sub-contractor or white labeling**—Still making it look like they own the technology but understanding that the external company could do it much better and faster than them.

5. **True collaboration**—Identifying and pursuing mutually beneficial partnerships that result in a win-win scenario for both parties. Such collaborations can only be achieved by working together closely and leveraging each other's strengths and resources to achieve a common goal.

Naturally, a company does not need to follow through all maturity levels and can jump ahead, but the more traditional it is, the harder it will become. The most mature companies might also have a mixture of all the above, looking at these options as various tool sets to utilize according to the opportunity and need. This is the best way for companies to manage technology integration by utilizing the best and most suitable framework as it sees fit.

For startups, it is essential to understand the phase in which a corporation is currently situated to avoid disappointments and setbacks along the way. Since startups typically operate with limited resources and narrow bandwidth, placing their bet on the wrong company could waste valuable time and money. However, it is important to note that this does not necessarily mean that the corporation is exploiting them for their needs. Instead, it could indicate a lack of maturity on the corporate side in terms of collaborating with external companies.

3.5 Internal Versus External—The Innovation Challenge

As mentioned, when a company decides to go down the path of innovation there is always tension between external and internal; should the company develop everything in-house or look for compatible solutions out there and work to integrate them as part of their product roadmap?

I would like to point out that there is no right or wrong here and the answer lies mostly in the culture of the organization and what is best for it, but I do want to emphasize the importance of a misconception in the external versus internal debate.

There are many companies that believe that the fact that they set up a key innovation role in their company or the fact that their engineers or product managers call themselves "innovation leaders," make them more innovative in some way, while this could not be further from the truth.

Innovation, as Steve Jobs put it, "is the ability to see change as an opportunity and not a threat." It is understanding that the world is changing, and you should change along with it.

The way I see it, a company that chooses to focus solely on internal innovation does not fully grasp the full potential out there. As a company, it is simply impossible to hold all the knowledge and inevitably there will be gaps and blind spots. This has become the harsh reality since products have become more and more digitalized and fragmentized.

A company that thinks it could do everything internally, might find itself veering away from the innovation path and focusing entirely on product development roadmap. Innovation quickly transforms into building new features for existing products.

This is the base of the misconception I would like to address: The point of Internal versus External is not necessarily self-development versus adopting external assistance and know-how, but whether the development is linked to the core of the company or not.

A few years ago, I had the opportunity to meet with the top management of a very large manufacturing company that had its own internal software engineering team. This team had developed their own Enterprise Resource Planning (ERP) system, which the company's management was extremely proud of. They saw no need to engage with external companies since they believed they had the capabilities to develop everything they needed in-house.

Taking this example, to my point, if the ERP system is part of the product, which you sell as a company, it is internal. However, when it is not a product component as such and its sole purpose is to support the deployment/development/management of the product, it is external know-how you bring into the company.

Following the logic above, if the manufacturing company will decide eventually to start selling the ERP system they have developed, then it will become core and internal, but as long as the ERP system is not an active component of the company's product suite itself, it is just supporting the core business and, thus, external to the company's focus. Then management could decide whether they use an external company for this or utilize their own team. Failing to understand the value of external know-how and explore such opportunities has the risk of misconception and eventually tying innovation to product enhancement, while believing you, as a company, are still at the front line of innovation.

Establishing an innovation team within the corporation, whose sole focus is to cultivate external global partnerships, collaborate with startups, and form research affiliations that accelerate the company's innovation vision, can be an effective innovation strategy.

This is particularly relevant when considering that the primary purpose of incorporating external expertise is to enrich and accelerate core activities. By avoiding any interference with the product development roadmaps managed by the core engineering team, an innovation team can aid internal development endeavors in rapidly incorporating technology partnerships that meet the company's innovation requirements. If a company lacks a clear and defined strategy for innovation, along with the right people to drive it, it is highly probable that they will fail on their path toward innovation.

Unfortunately, it is a sad truth that many companies do tend to fail along this transformation process and might confuse the reasons for failure, as I will cover in the chapter ahead.

CHAPTER 4

Why Do Companies Find It So Hard to Innovate

Many companies struggle with the implementation of new technologies, and as previously discussed, the larger and more traditional the company, the more challenging the process can become.

It is not uncommon for successful entrepreneurs to attempt to apply their knowledge and expertise to new domains, only to find that they face significant challenges when trying to establish connections with traditional corporations. Overall, innovation requires a willingness to take risks, invest in research and development, embrace change, and foster a culture of creativity and experimentation. Companies that are able to overcome these barriers and prioritize innovation are more likely to succeed in today's rapidly changing business environment.

4.1 The DNA of Large Corporations

Large corporations tend to struggle when it comes to incorporating innovation due to their complex and bureaucratic structures. The process of introducing innovative practices can feel like redirecting an aircraft carrier down a river, particularly for more traditional and older companies that could be more resistant to change.

Large corporations are usually very hierarchal but still have a multi-layer decision process, which means a decision is not taken by one person but rather a group of people working together from various teams. After reaching a decision, they present it to upper management for approval.

The organizational structures within a large corporation are designed to facilitate the company's strategic objectives and ensure smooth operations with clear lines of responsibility and accountability. Employees typically work within specific departments or business units, each with its own goals and targets. Large corporations also have access to substantial resources, such as financial capital, intellectual property, and highly skilled personnel, which can be used to achieve their objectives. However, the complexity of these organizations creates challenges, particularly in terms of communication, collaboration, and the ability to adapt to changing circumstances. Moreover, the budgeting process is typically predetermined, and each division's budget is based on a presubmitted plan from its management. As a result, there is limited flexibility for adjustments throughout the year, making it difficult to adapt and change according to changing circumstances.

The implementation of decisions made by executives can be hindered by bureaucratic processes if employees choose to ignore or delay the decision until a new manager takes over. Therefore, it is crucial to gain the buy-in and support of all parties involved to ensure successful implementation. A wise manager will therefore not override the decisions of their employees, but instead, work to guide them toward the desired outcome and facilitate their understanding of the decision and its implications. This approach can increase the likelihood of successful implementation and maintain positive relationships with the team, as the manager depends on their support to achieve success.

In general, employees in a large corporation can be categorized into three main groups:

- **People who focus solely on the politics**—These are the vocal people, trying to get noticed and from the moment they wake up to the moment they go to sleep they work solely on how to advance themselves, become noticeable and at the center of attention. I am a strong believer in the phrase: "actions speaks louder than words" and for this group, it is the other way around.
- **People who work at not being noticeable**—The total opposite to the above. These people try as much as they can not to become noticeable and hope that no one looks too deep into what they do on a day to day.
- **People who focus on the work**—These are the people who focus on the work that should be done and hate the politics game. The adept ones comprehend the significance of political

maneuvering but view it as an essential tool for advancement, exercising it accordingly as needed. In contrast, those who are not as skilled tend to shy away from the limelight and are less likely to ascend the corporate hierarchy.

The impact of corporate politics is evident in the different approaches of startups and corporate business development professionals toward achieving their goals, or the difference between "what" and "how." Start-ups focus on developing a clear message and determining the best way to deliver it to their audience, while corporate business development professionals focus on creating a strategy for delivering the message effectively to relevant stakeholders while taking into account political considerations.

Unfortunately, politics is an inherent aspect of large corporations due to their hierarchical structure, which creates power imbalances and uneven distribution of resources. As a result, decision-making could be often influenced by personal relationships, status, and informal networks, leading to political maneuvering and power struggles.

4.2 Failure to Incorporate Innovation

Although innovation is an important component of business success, many companies still struggle to consistently incorporate new and innovative ideas. There are numerous factors that can contribute to a company's failure to innovate, including:

1. **Fear of Failure**

   One of the biggest barriers to innovation is the fear of failure. Many companies are risk-averse and prioritize stability and predictability over experimentation and innovation. This can lead to a culture that discourages creativity and punishes failure, making it difficult for new ideas to gain traction.

   Therefore, in order to overcome traditional thinking and foster innovation, companies should seek diversity and a range of perspectives to challenge established norms. Conversely, companies with limited diversity may find it increasingly difficult to shift their mindset and embrace innovative practices.

To foster a culture of experimentation and learning, it is important for companies to encourage employees to take calculated risks, recognize and reward innovation efforts, and establish a process for evaluating and learning from failures and setbacks. These steps can help create a culture of innovation that supports continuous learning and improvement.

2. Putting the Wrong Person in Place

The first tendency of large corporations is to nominate someone internally to lead the innovation initiative, under the assumption that it will be easier for someone who already knows the corporate organization and is familiar with internal politics and stakeholders. Although in some cases this person could have the right mindset and could potentially grow into the role, in many other cases it is just the wrong person who is already "tainted" with the corporate mindset and process and simply does not have what it takes to think outside the box.

In some cases, this can even result in internal conflicts if the business units are not convinced of the capabilities of the nominated leader or if the leader fails to adequately explain the goal of his team.

Being an innovation manager or leading an innovation team takes a different skill set; it is more about how to push things forward and be a mediator between the corporation and the external engagements. In addition, it is crucial for the manager of such a team to possess the necessary expertise and experience to select the right team members and provide them with effective guidance and mentorship.

3. Frequently Changing the Structure

Naturally, when things do not work out well, the first tendency is to change the structure and strategy over and over. Some companies may even focus excessively on the process, striving for perfection, without realizing the importance of other elements such as the team.

I have found out that the right team with the wrong process would still be much more effective than the wrong team with the right process.

Frequent changes in the upper management do not help too, since whenever there is a new executive, he might try to change the entire strategy instead of just letting the innovation team do what they do best.

In many cases, the company does not understand what it takes to truly onboard innovation and focuses only on finding the right ideas, without addressing the need to implement them. Changing the structure when you lack this basic understanding, or when you have no real strategy behind, will not address the root cause, and keep on changing the less critical elements around.

This lack of understanding is particularly apparent during difficult times, when innovation departments are often the first to be cut. However, this short-sighted approach can hinder the company's long-term growth, as there will be no one left to manage and implement innovative ideas. It is like going on a diet by cutting off your leg; you will lose the weight, but it will leave you without a leg to stand on in the long run.

4. **Short-Term Thinking**

Innovation efforts can take time to yield results, and traditional corporations may prioritize short-term results since they focus on revenues and Return on Investment (ROI) over long-term innovation efforts. In some cases, it will also be extremely hard to measure the immediate impact since some of the innovation team goals are less quantitative, like increasing innovation mindset and awareness, stakeholders' satisfaction or having synchronization among the various teams.

However, it is also very important that innovation efforts have clear goals and metrics to track progress and measure success, since without them, innovation efforts can become unfocused and ineffective. Therefore, it is important to have a right mix and balance between both quantitative and qualitative Key Performance Indicators (KPIs) for such a team.

Examples of quantitative Key Performance Indicators (KPIs) may include metrics such as the number of Proof of Concepts (POCs) conducted and their specific focus within a particular division, the number of engagements or investments made, or even more basic tasks such as onboarding external companies and summarizing those engagements within the Customer Relationship Management (CRM) system.

To be truly effective, leaders must find the right balance between achieving short-term results and pursuing long-term innovation objectives. Failing to achieve this balance can result in a lack of focus and hinder the team's ability to achieve its goals.

5. **Losing the Champion Within the Corporation**

   Having a champion within the organization is essential to ensure that initiatives move forward and do not fall through the cracks. Given that in order to proceed, you will need the buy of more than a few people in various positions, a person who is high enough in the company's hierarchy and who could coordinate and push things forward, could mean the difference between success and getting stuck along the process. Losing this key team member can quickly derail progress, especially if the company fails to find a suitable replacement. Even if there is a dedicated innovation team responsible for promoting new initiatives, they will still need to identify and collaborate with key champions within the business units they work with. The main focus of the innovation team will be to function as a liaison between these business units and external companies. In the absence of leadership helping to steer these engagements forward, day-to-day challenges can take priority, causing future innovation projects to be deprioritized.

6. **Focusing on the Failures**

   A company will surely face some failures along the way. The importance is to learn from these failures so that the ratio of success increases. Focusing on the failures would just mean that people will become less convicted in the innovation program and team, and this team could consequently lose the internal backing.

7. **Resistance to Change**

   Resistance to change, or Not Invented Here (NIH) syndrome is one of the biggest challenges to overcome. Large and traditional corporate cultures can be resistant to change, either because they think they know better or simply because people are intimidated by any change, making it difficult to adopt new ideas and concepts.

   The more traditional and well established the corporation is, the more experts will feel that they can do everything by themselves, and that the outside world has less to educate them. Experts will therefore most likely be overly critical to new ideas from the outside world when these are presented to them and might even try to hamper any attempts to do so. As I will share later, there are various methods to overcome this issue, such as working through the pain points or leveraging the know-how from other sectors.

8. **Ignoring Market Trends**

Ignoring market trends and failing to adapt to changing customer needs and preferences is a common mistake. Failing to follow market trends can result in developing products or services that do not meet customer needs or are out of touch with the current market. As discussed earlier, conducting comprehensive market research and analysis is essential for avoiding this mistake. This involves identifying emerging trends, evolving customer needs, and new market opportunities, which can help the company stay ahead of the curve and maintain a competitive edge. The company should also engage with customers and stakeholders to gather feedback and insights regarding their needs and preferences. By staying attuned to market trends and customer requirements, the company can develop innovative solutions that meet customer needs, create value, and drive growth. Failing to do so could become the difference between growth and extinction all together and companies like Kodak, Nokia, and Blockbuster are great examples for disregarding, or being too slow to act on such changes.

9. **Lack of Leadership Commitment**

Leadership plays a crucial role in promoting innovation within an organization. Leaders must create a culture of innovation that encourages and rewards creativity, risk-taking, and collaboration. This requires setting a clear vision and strategy for innovation, communicating this vision effectively to employees, and providing the necessary resources and support to achieve it. Stating that your organization is promoting innovation, is totally worthless without the proper backing. Of course, it is important to have the right team in place, but you will need reassurances and the willingness from business units to experiment too. Leaving this to be figured out by the innovation team could get you a step further down the road, but it would be much slower and less efficient than if the business units understand that this is what the top management is expecting.

Having a skilled team in the right hierarchical position within the organization is undoubtedly beneficial, but it is not enough on its own. As I will cover in the following chapter, further actions are required to ensure that the team is effectively leveraged and that their expertise is utilized to its full potential.

Leaders must also lead by example and demonstrate their commitment to innovation through their actions and decisions. They should encourage and empower employees to generate new ideas, experiment with new approaches, and challenge the status quo.

It is crucial for business units to recognize the importance of innovation and experimentation and the only way to ensure this, is by incorporating it into their Key Performance Indicators (KPIs) or compensation plan. Without this linkage, the initiative may be perceived as less of a priority by the business units and could result in a lack of buy-in from their side.

One effective approach that I have encountered involved setting aside a specific portion of each business unit's budget for innovation. This portion of the budget could only be used for innovation initiatives, and if it were not utilized, the funds were forfeited. As a result, each business unit was incentivized to maximize their use of this budget and invest in innovation initiatives. Not surprisingly, every business unit exploited this portion to the limit.

10. Siloed Thinking

Traditional corporate structures can be siloed, with departments or teams working in isolation. These could be simply because the departments are totally different from each other and belong to different divisions or because the management pushes for competition among teams. Innovation requires cross-functional collaboration and breaking down silos to enable collaboration and knowledge sharing across different departments or teams within an organization.

11. Failure to involve Employees

It is important to recognize that internal employees are a valuable source of innovative ideas and should be actively included in innovation efforts. At the end of the day, they are the ones who have the deepest understanding of the company, which enables them to come up with the most efficient and optimal solutions to tackle any challenge. By involving employees in the innovation process, companies can increase engagement, boost job satisfaction, and enhance problem-solving skills. This can lead to a greater sense of value and motivation among employees, ultimately contributing to the company's goals. Neglecting to involve employees can result in missed opportunities and a lack of commitment. Some companies might try to address this by internal incubation or ideation programs, but if these programs lack the sufficient funding, backing or the right team to lead them, they will go nowhere.

12. **Lack of Collaboration With External Partners**
   Innovation often requires collaboration with external partners, such as startups, accelerators, or academic institutions, as it allows companies to access new knowledge, technologies, and expertise that may not be available in-house. Failing to collaborate and not being able to become part of the community effectively can therefore limit access to new ideas and technologies.

To highlight the importance of recognizing the challenges in integrating innovation in the corporate world, I would like to share the following example: A multinational corporation my friend represented, decided to expand its local operations from scouting to an innovation hub, with the support of the CEO and the recruitment of a team of engineers. Although the move seemed promising at first, the company eventually decided to shut down the hub after a few years. Sadly, this is not an uncommon occurrence in the corporate world, as I myself had been hired and then let go after only two months due to a change in the company's strategy.

Upon analyzing the corporation's decision with my friend, we identified the following reasons for the change:

- The decision to open the hub lacked a clear strategy, as it followed the visit of the CEO and was not accompanied by a well-defined strategic plan.

- The person appointed to oversee the local hub was the Chief Information Security Officer (CISO) rather than someone from the corporate's business units who had a more direct connection to the product.
- The corporate decided to invest in a local startup in parallel, with the idea of utilizing their capabilities for developing future technological solutions. However, the technological due diligence of the startup was not executed by a team with knowledge of the business and product side of the corporation. The first task assigned to the local startup was to evaluate one of the corporate's business units, which led to animosity toward both the startup and the local operation.
- Despite multiple visits by the headquarters to the innovation hub, no managers from the product side of the business units ever visited. The visits that did take place were focused more on scouting technologies and innovation.
- There was confusion over leadership, as two heads were nominated, one for administrative and local technology scouting tasks and the other for the technical team, yet there was no clear understanding of who held the primary leadership role.
- Insufficient internal PR led to many business units being unaware of the operation, its capabilities, technical knowhow, and its purpose.

Ultimately, the decision to expand the operations to an innovation hub was the right call, but the execution was poor, lacking clear strategy, leadership, and backing from relevant teams of the corporation, which ultimately led to the decision to shut down the local operation.

As evident, there are numerous challenges that organizations may face when trying to integrate innovation into their operations. It is therefore imperative to identify and address these obstacles while establishing a solid foundation and strategy for the successful implementation of innovative ideas.

CHAPTER 5

Establishing the Right Foundation

In order to ensure that your organization is on the right path for innovation and is valued so by external companies, it is vital to establish a strong foundation consisting of the right process, the right team members, and the right mindset.

5.1 Building the Right Process

It is not enough for companies to simply claim that they are innovative. They need to invest funds and resources to identify interesting solutions and experiment with them. Therefore, being able to analyze, filter, and onboard new solutions is crucial for the success of such activities. As discussed, this can become particularly challenging for large and traditional companies, which are often calibrated to work with either vendors or customers.

To overcome these challenges, it is essential to put the right framework in place. This framework should help these companies to figure out where they should focus and how to evaluate new ideas and implement them as quickly and agile as possible. Eventually, this will make the whole difference between success and just burning through money.

The framework should include clear guidelines for evaluating new ideas and solutions, as well as a process for testing and implementing them.

Furthermore, corporations should invest in the right talent and technology to enable them to effectively evaluate, filter, and onboard new solutions and external companies. This may include hiring experts in innovation and emerging technologies, as well as investing in software and other technology tools that can help streamline the evaluation and onboarding process.

Here are some of the key metrics to consider while putting this process in place:

- **A dedicated team**—for onboarding innovation. In case there are a few teams focused on innovation, such as an investment or M&A team, it is important to define boundaries and areas of responsibility, to avoid confusion and miscommunication.
- **A clear mandate** from the management to lead this topic and experiment.
- **Clear strategy**—clear goals and objectives for innovation.
- **The right hierarchy and positioning**—the people within the dedicated team should have the right experience and the ranking to support it, reporting to top management.
- **Budget and resources**—to support POCs and experimentation with innovative initiatives.
- **Clear onboarding process**—dedicated toward POCs, enabling the testing of external technologies which differs from the onboarding of regular vendors. This process should include clear guidelines for evaluating potential partners, as well as a dedicated process for testing and implementing new ideas and should be mutually agreed upon by all stakeholders.
- **Statement of Work (SOW)**—the company should have a transparent and comprehensive evaluation procedure for new external ideas. This process should include the description of the test itself, KPIs for success, designated timelines, and resources needed.
- **Establishing clear communication**—clear communication channels and protocols to ensure that both parties are aligned and informed throughout the collaboration. For example, defining a project manager from each side and setting up a weekly call to cover the progress and address the challenges.
- **Measuring and monitoring progress**—throughout the collaboration to ensure that it is on track to achieve its objectives. This can help identify areas for improvement and make adjustments as needed. However, it is equally important to understand when to make the decision to move on or not.

- **Define the ownership and Intellectual Property (IP) rights**—that are related to the partnership and may arise from the collaboration. As I will elaborate in chapter 7, this topic may be less of an issue during the POC phase, as it mainly involves evaluating the technology at hand. However, it will become important to address this topic when moving forward, particularly in cases where there is collaboration to tailor the solution to the organization's specific needs, which could potentially lead to the development of a new solution.

If the collaboration is not meeting the established objectives and is not showing signs of improvement, it may be time to consider ending the partnership. The company should have clear criteria for evaluating the success of the collaboration and make decisions based on those criteria.

In addition, the company should also evaluate the benefits and costs of the collaboration on an ongoing basis. If the costs outweigh the benefits, it may be time to reevaluate the collaboration or consider ending it.

Making the decision to move on or not can be difficult, especially if there are sunk costs or relationships involved. However, it is important to prioritize objectives and make decisions based on what is best for the organization.

In order to avoid becoming opportunistic and to ensure that collaborations with external partners are focused and purposeful, the dedicated innovation team should spend time with the business units and understand their needs. By doing so, they can develop a game plan for focus fields and targets that align with the overall business strategy and goals.

This game plan should include clear criteria for evaluating potential partners, as well as a process for evaluating and selecting partners based on their expertise, track record, and cultural fit. It should also include a clear communication plan and protocols to ensure that both parties are aligned and informed throughout the collaboration.

5.2 Building the Right Team

Corporations might nominate a veteran employee who lacks the relevant know-how and experience, to lead innovation, thinking that this will expedite things within the organization, failing to understand that this should be treated as a profession by itself. As discussed, instead of nominating the right person and building the right team around them, they might revert to changing the process over and over.

Moreover, there is always a tension between leading innovation activities by internal business units or rather a corporate dedicated team, and finding the right balance is therefore crucial.

When assembling an innovation team, a common question that arises is how extensive their technical knowledge should be.

On the one hand, these teams need to display a good technical understanding since they are the gateway and first filter for the corporation, working closely with internal technical teams, but on the other hand, they should establish a good relationship and trust with both the companies they bring onboard and the internal stakeholders, which might require a totally different tool set.

The answer is not that simple, and many innovation leaders contemplate on what is the right balance to make a team as efficient and successful as possible. Some tend to mold the team in their own image, and some strive to create a better balance and the right mixture of various talents.

When I built my team, I had a very clear image of what I am looking for:

First of all, I was looking for **curiosity and passion**; you cannot push innovation without being curious and wanting to learn and educate yourself, or without the passion to do so. Secondly, the team members should be **self-sufficient** and know how to educate themselves with no corporate support. If the expectation is to learn and understand new topics that might be outside the comfort zone of the organization, the team members must know how to do so. Then, it was important to find people who have **the right balance**, not too technical but enough to have a technical conversation with technical teams, while being a people's person. Therefore, instead of finding the balance within the team, I looked for the right balance within each individual team member. Of course, some could be more technical and some more on the people person side, but the balance should be there.

In my opinion, it is more important for the team members to understand this balance rather than attempting to outsmart the professionals they work with, as this may not always be the most practical approach. Therefore, rather than investing time in mastering a particular subject in great technical detail, they should invest the time to comprehend and understand the professionals' needs.

The reasoning behind this is that you can never have a better technical understanding than the people who have been doing this for so many years. Hence, you need to find a way to have a good relationship with them without posing a threat, while building bridges to the outside world. This is a fine balance, and you should maneuver it smartly. Therefore, my motto has always been **to learn a bit on everything from the people who know everything on one thing.** This way you will be able to leverage your know-how and connect the dots between various technologies, sectors, and people.

Moreover, when you give the other party the feeling that you are contributing something to them while simultaneously being eager to learn from them, they will be more inclined to share their knowledge and establish a genuine partnership.

And here comes one of the most interesting attributes you need to look for; your team members should be great **storytellers,** as discussed previously. A storyteller understands and reads his audience, knowing how to adjust and tell the story in the right way that will attract and thrill them. He needs to understand what is interesting to them and how to drive them to action.

Eventually, it is not just about understanding the technology and being able to connect the dots, but how to get the other side more enthusiastic and bring him on board to support you actively along the journey.

Another key factor for the success of such a team is **diversity**. A diverse team from various cultures and backgrounds can provide a broader range of perspectives and experiences that can help the company to identify new opportunities and develop innovative solutions. Additionally, diversity can help the company to better understand and serve a diverse customer base. While managing a diverse team can be challenging, with a good manager who is able to keep the team focused, diversity can be leveraged to increase knowledge and reach for the corporation.

5.3 Building the Right Mindset

It is not only important to understand that you need to experiment and be open to learn from external companies but also crucial to have the endorsement of top executives and adequate resources set aside for this purpose.

These top executives must share a common understanding that innovation requires time to achieve success and instead of consistently seeking an ROI and altering the structure, they should concentrate on creating the proper team and providing the right framework and support. Having the top management simply state that they are driving innovation is not enough and this should be embedded in the business units' budget plan and strategy.

Leveraging external solutions that address the corporation's needs is a nice start but eventually not sufficient and a company that wants to become more innovative and encourage innovation within the company should work on internal initiatives as well.

Various teams should have the opportunity to experiment and participate in external events to open their minds to various possibilities. They should be given the mandate to take ownership of innovation initiatives and have the autonomy to make decisions. This can help create a sense of ownership and accountability that can drive innovation.

Some companies might even take this a step further and have internal incubation programs, corporate innovation hubs, or company builders. They might even encourage and support their employees' entrepreneurial ambitions by providing financial backing and other resources to establish their own startups, particularly for ideas that the corporation could not support internally. This approach allows companies to retain talented employees and potentially benefit from the success of their startups while simultaneously fostering a culture of innovation and entrepreneurship within the organization.

Even if the corporation does not provide active support for employees' entrepreneurial ambitions, it is still important to foster a culture of innovation. Therefore, corporations should encourage collaboration and support cross-functional teams across various business units. This can help bring together diverse perspectives and expertise to solve complex problems and develop innovative solutions.

Another important path is to have the company experts become involved in the outside world as mentors or advisors to accelerators or incubation programs. This is of course a great win-win when these programs could provide their teams with know-how and experience and the experts to be exposed to the outside world and what is happening in the innovation landscape beyond their company.

Opening new company hubs at designated locations around the globe is also a great way to incorporate the innovation spirit and educate internal employees, by having visits and exchange programs. This will create a more diversified spirit and help the company educate its internal employees on what is out there.

Here are a few ideas you can start implementing to foster the innovation spirit within your company:

1. **Workshops**—One effective way to foster creativity and idea generation is through workshops. These workshops should be focused on a specific topic and attended by various teams within the organization. To ensure maximum participation and diverse perspectives, it is important to keep the workshops as lean as possible. Ideally, workshops should have no more than 10 to 15 people who are relevant to the topic from various units within the organization. the workshops should be facilitated by a skilled facilitator who can guide the discussion, encourage participation, and ensure that everyone's ideas are heard.

   Conducting workshops can be an effective approach to addressing a common pain point across the organization, especially since meeting each stakeholder individually may result in rejection. By bringing together people who face similar challenges in a single room, it can emphasize and accelerate willingness to collaborate on the matter.

2. **Cross-functional task force**—In larger organizations, it is not uncommon to find various teams addressing the same problem or working on similar projects in silos. By creating cross-functional teams, employees can share knowledge, collaborate on shared problems, and share solutions they are currently utilizing. To ensure the success of these task forces, it is important to select experts from various teams who have a deep understanding of the matter at hand. For example, a manufacturing company that operates multiple plants

and is focused on implementing industry 4.0 initiatives, should form a cross-functional task force consisting of experts in manufacturing, engineering, technology, and other relevant areas.

These task forces should be given clear objectives and goals and be provided with the resources and support they need to achieve them. The task forces should also be encouraged to think outside the box and come up with innovative solutions to the problems they are addressing. In addition, it is important to provide a platform for the task forces to share their findings and recommendations with the wider organization. This can be achieved via regular meetings, reports, or presentations to senior management.

3. **Participating at innovation global events**—Attending innovation-focused events is another effective strategy for fostering creativity and idea generation within an organization. Global events that focus on innovation can invigorate employees and help them step out of their comfort zone. If the organization has multiple locations around the world, the person leading innovation within each region should be given the task of hosting a delegation to attend events in their region. These events should be diverse yet effective in bringing together a group of employees from various units within the organization.

To ensure maximum participation and engagement, it is important to map out the events in advance and provide opportunities for rotating the attendees. These events should not be treated as tourist attractions, but rather as opportunities for the teams to come up with new ideas or partnerships they would like to explore post-event. The expectation should be that participants come up with a few concrete ideas or partnerships that they would like to explore post the event.

By setting this expectation, attendees will be more engaged and focused during the event, actively seeking out new ideas and partnerships that align with their objectives.

4. **Provide training**—Companies should provide training on creative thinking and idea generation, which could be conducted by internal experts or external trainers.

One effective training method is to run hackathons that are mentored by internal experts around a specific topic. Hackathons are intense brainstorming sessions where teams work together to develop solutions to a specific problem. These sessions are typically time-boxed and can last for a few hours or a few days, depending on the complexity of the problem.

By providing training on creative thinking and idea generation, companies can equip employees with the tools they need, to come up with innovative solutions and drive business growth. In addition, hackathons and other training sessions can help foster collaboration and knowledge sharing among teams and across generations, which can lead to the development of new ideas and solutions.

5. **Encourage feedback**—Encouraging feedback is an important strategy for refining and improving ideas within an organization. One effective way to encourage feedback is to have teams develop a new concept and present it at an annual event where all other employees and top management come to see what they have developed. This provides a sense of prestige and pride and pushes teams to participate and come up with new ideas.

This annual event can be a platform for teams to showcase their ideas and receive feedback from a diverse group of people within the organization. The feedback received can help refine and improve the ideas and provide an opportunity for collaboration and improvement.

Eventually, fostering a culture of innovation requires a commitment from the management and a change of mindset of the organization to encourage experimentation, provide resources, recognize, and reward innovation, empower employees, and foster collaboration. By creating a culture of innovation, companies can stay ahead of the curve and achieve long-term success.

CHAPTER 6

Different Paths to Incorporate External Innovation

Once a company has established the appropriate framework and mindset, they may consider the most efficient approach to integrate external knowledge into their operations. There are multiple practices for integrating external innovation into a company, each with its own advantages and disadvantages. The most suitable option will depend on the company's perspective, goals, and available resources.

6.1 Build Versus Buy

In today's rapidly evolving business landscape, traditional companies that have become accustomed to developing everything in-house may face significant challenges in adapting to the changing times. As the world continues to evolve, it is essential for these companies to recognize that relying solely on internal resources may no longer be sustainable or efficient.

The company therefore may choose to have a combination of various teams working on internal solutions and those working on bringing in external solutions. However, when a company is in the early stages of exploring external solutions, it may be more inclined to maintain control over the technology. This often involves acquiring the external company entirely or utilizing them as a subcontractor, thereby ensuring a certain level of ownership and control over the technology.

The most common practice of buying an external company is known as Mergers and Acquisitions (M&A). This refers to the process of combining two or more companies into a single entity. M&A transactions can take several forms, including mergers, acquisitions, and divestitures.

Mergers occur when two companies combine to form a new entity, while acquisitions involve one company purchasing another. Divestitures refer to the sale or spin-off of a business unit or subsidiary.

The M&A process typically involves several stages, including strategic planning, target identification, due diligence (evaluating the target company's financial, legal, and operational performance), negotiation, and integration.

M&A offers several advantages, such as the opportunity to expand the market share and diversify into new sectors, resulting in cost-saving synergies, and access to new markets. Additionally, M&A can provide an opportunity for talent acquisition, bringing in skilled professionals who can contribute innovative solutions to the company's operations and promote diversification.

However, the integration of one company into another is always a challenging process that can many times result in failure. Often, the failure is due to people's resistance, either from the acquired company struggling to adapt to the corporate mentality or in-house personnel who are concerned about the changes. The acquired company may find it difficult to operate under the corporate bureaucracy, which can stifle their creativity and innovation. This can lead to frustration and ultimately, the failure of the M&A integration.

6.2 Invest—Corporate Venture Capital (CVC)

A corporate investment into a startup could be a great approach and therefore a CVC is a great tool for corporations to accelerate innovation and achieve financial returns at the same time. In contrast to traditional methods like M&A, it enables you to spread your bets without spending too much, spot the next tech wave ahead of the competition, and work with fast teams without suffocating them under the corporate umbrella. The startup gets access, knowledge, and a strong partner to go to market with.

For these reasons, many of those corporations looking to jump-start their Innovation activities have launched their own CVC programs.

A quick look at the CVC landscape will most likely reveal a mix of organizational setups with vague mandates that tend to mix up strategic/

operational and financial goals. This is, in many cases, due to the fact that the CVC setup evolved from the corporate's innovation life cycle rather than the outcome of a full strategic and structured plan for investments.

Therefore, having a well-defined approach to establishing a CVC team is crucial to ensure that the team can effectively support the company's future objectives.

As covered in Chapter 3, after following the Not Invented Here (NIH) phase, the company usually comes to an understanding that they cannot do everything internally and look and experiment at buying companies to own the technology. Then they come to the understanding that this is not a sustainable practice and the companies it bought might not execute well under the corporate umbrella.

The next stage entails recognizing that acquiring the entire company may not be necessary when one can make an investment and still receive almost the same benefits.

This is where things can get complicated; determining how to structure a CVC unit that effectively addresses the corporation's strategic requirements while ensuring the operation is sustainable and set up for long-term success.

6.2.1 The Challenge

On one hand, it is essential to avoid having the Key Performance Indicators (KPIs) of the CVC team solely focused on strategic objectives. If the team only focuses on strategic KPIs, they may invest in many innovative ideas, but could eventually find themselves without viable companies to deliver them. Simply having a great idea is not sufficient to guarantee a company's success and for a company to succeed, it must have the ability to independently grow and develop its products while securing adequate funding to do so. However, even if the company becomes financially successful, the return on investment of a few million dollars into a startup may not significantly impact a multi-billion-dollar organization.

Furthermore, strategic KPIs are subject to change and can be inconsistent. If the CVC team's investment behavior changes due to shifts in the strategy of internal business units, they may not develop a consistent investment practice that is taken seriously by the ecosystem. At the same time, focusing solely on financial KPIs may result in a portfolio of financially attractive deals that have no real connection to the corporation's activities and are of no use for the advancement of the company's innovation efforts.

6.2.2 The Solution

The best approach therefore is to leverage both worlds. It is crucial to remember that investing in a company is just one method of gaining access to new ideas and technology. Additionally, pursuing these KPIs with one team is nearly impossible, which is why you will need two:

I. CVC investment management

For the CVC to become successful it is essential to have a team that includes individuals with extensive financial expertise and a solid technical understanding. They should focus solely on the investment procedure and execution. They will sit in the company's board if needed and agreed upon and will help steer it toward financial success.

The sole goal of the CVC team should be financial, and this team will need to make sure that they are executing the right investments that make sense financially so that the startup will have a future.

Eventually, you need good financial people who know what they are doing and set the right valuation and framework with the company that will not jeopardize its future fundraising and development.

II. Operational team

Then, you should have a separate designated team that should focus on the operational side and try utilizing the internal resources to help grow the startups you invested in as a partner in a win-win situation.

As I see it, it is never a good idea to mix operational and financial in one place, since you then get a team that is confused on what is expected from them, and when they are confused, the management and the outside world will get confused too.

This could even jeopardize the company's reputation. Consider a scenario where a company is attempting to validate a new technology. The business unit finds two great startups they want to evaluate and then the CVC team comes up with a third one they think is great. If the CVC team becomes too heavily involved in the process, the first two companies may feel that the corporation is exploiting them to gain knowledge to invest in the third company. In the same manner, if someone from the operations sits on the startup's board, he can potentially steer the company to what is best for the corporation rather than to the startup's best interest.

Therefore, the best way is to have a separate and designated operational team that deals with all operations and a CVC team that deals with investments and postinvestment portfolio management. This sets the clear boundaries, thus reducing the friction and "stepping on the toes" of the other team.

This does not mean that both teams should not work together, on the contrary. When working closely together, the CVC could also follow through on operational collaborations after the technology has been validated and a product market fit is found. This will reduce the risk of investment and make sure the corporation enjoys the value it generates to the startup.

While the CVC KPIs must be financially driven, it is essential to ensure that they align with the corporation's strategy. One way to achieve this is to set up an investment committee that will have the final say.

The investment committee should have the right balance and mix of leaders from the organization that are aligned with the strategy and could also look at things from a high-level position while still being able to maintain a good understanding of the difficulties and challenges that lie ahead.

The importance of the CVC to the corporation is to get a foot in the door, and leverage bets in technologies and solutions that will make sense to the company, but they should also have the freedom to make investments that are for the long term and are not yet on the clear path of the corporation. In this way, they will turn to a real true spearhead and keep the company on the right track toward innovation. They should work very closely with the operational team as well as the business units and be the final say in everything related to a financial investment without getting involved in the operational activities and therefore should be measured only according to financial KPIs.

Knowing how to structure the CVC unit effectively can help overcome potential disadvantages such as confusion in expectations, conflicts of interest, and consistency. This understanding will enable companies to leverage CVC investments in the most optimal way and achieve their innovation targets efficiently.

6.3 Partner—Building Technology Partnerships

The choice to partner with an external company is the more mature choice usually, coming from an understanding that an external company could add as much value as they can receive from the partnership. The challenge is to find the exact stage that makes sense; on the one hand, a company with know-how and a proven solution and on the other hand, small enough so they could still see the partnership as one that could benefit them.

These partnerships could come in many formats, but the most known ones are:

- **Strategic alliances**—Forming strategic alliances with partners that can provide access to new markets, technologies, or resources.
- **Joint ventures**—Generating collaborative partnerships to pursue specific business opportunities, such as developing new products or entering new markets.
- **Licensing and franchising**—Licensing intellectual property or franchising business models to partners to expand market reach and generate revenue.
- **Supplier and vendor partnerships**—Building partnerships with suppliers and vendors to improve the quality and reliability of goods and services and reduce costs.
- **Co-creation and co-innovation**—Collaborating with partners to co-create and co-innovate products or services that meet customer needs and solve problems.

Co-creation and co-innovation with external partners are effective ways to drive innovation by leveraging external expertise and resources. It involves collaborating with external partners to develop and implement new products, services, or processes in a win-win model.

To leverage co-innovation and co-creation, the company should establish partnerships with external partners that have complementary skills, expertise, and resources. The company should also establish clear goals, timelines, and expectations for the collaboration, and be prepared to invest resources, such as time, funding, and talent, to support the collaboration.

By leveraging co-innovation and co-creation, companies are able to access new ideas and perspectives, reduce costs and risks, and accelerate the innovation process. They can also build stronger relationships with customers and suppliers and enhance their reputation as innovative companies.

Many corporations tend to focus on startups when seeking external know-how, assuming they have already figured out most of their needs and require assistance only with specific aspects. Although this might be the case on many occasions, these corporations are missing a much bigger opportunity of collaborating with larger companies. This might be more complex given things like compliance, but the harsh truth is that most companies simply do not know how to engage with other large corporations that are not automatically labeled under supplier or customer. If they do try to do so eventually, it remains on a low level or just via the salespeople they know. It is not about just getting to the right company; you need to get to the right person on the proper level as well. This has been the unfortunate truth for almost every company I worked with, and it never ceased to surprise me that I frequently found myself making connections among various people who are part of companies that have been in commercial connections for decades.

There are various examples of partnerships, such as:

- Two companies, each with a strong and established presence in different geographical markets, can collaborate to expand their reach and capitalize on new opportunities.
- An external company can license its technology to a well-known brand, allowing the brand to leverage the technology's benefits without having to develop it in-house.

- Two companies operating in the same market segment but offering different products can pool their resources and expertise to develop a cohesive end-to-end solution.
- An innovative startup can partner with a company possessing robust manufacturing expertise.
- A hardware solution provider can collaborate with a software company to offer a complete solution.
- A company and its customer can collaborate with a third party to facilitate a pilot project.
- A company that engages with its customers to offer ideas and new products. Lego, for example, has a program called "Lego Ideas," which allows customers to submit their own ideas for new Lego sets.

Establishing the right partnerships can significantly benefit a company's endeavors. it is therefore crucial to understand what the company is looking for and how to establish these relationships effectively. This is particularly important when the company has limited experience in generating such partnerships and is concerned about losing control, flexibility, and adapting to shared decision making and profit-sharing.

There are multiple approaches for incorporating external innovation into a company, each with its own benefits and drawbacks. However, deciding whether to develop an innovation internally or utilize external resources is not a straightforward decision and depends on various factors, including the availability of resources, expertise, and timing. In other words, does the company have the necessary time, resources, and expertise to develop the solution internally.

Selecting the right path for incorporating an external solution is a highly individual decision that must align with the company's unique needs and opportunities. Experienced and mature companies often have a range of options and specialized teams in place to select the best approach for each situation, providing them with the flexibility to choose the optimal solution. It is therefore crucial to assess the challenges, advantages, and disadvantages of each path to make the decision that could best cater the company's needs.

CHAPTER 7

Phases Toward Implementation

When a company finally decides to devote resources and explore external technologies, it is important for it to understand that looking for the right match, or scouting, is the easier part and it is what you do with it afterward that counts. Therefore, once a company has invested significant time and resources in establishing the appropriate structure and strategy, it becomes necessary to gain a comprehensive understanding of the onboarding process.

In order to implement an external solution, there are three phases to follow: internal examination and defining what you are looking for, external exploration, and finally, the implementation phase itself.

Each one of these phases is linked to the previous one, and therefore, in order to successfully implement a solution, each phase should be executed in the right way.

7.1 Phase 1—Internal Examination Into the Core

The ability to look at core activities of any operation and analyze it is the basis for any successful business development. The reasoning is that one cannot determine the long-term value of a company without gaining a comprehensive understanding of its fundamental operations and activities first. The analysis part comes once you understand the flow of operations and identify the challenges along the way.

In my view, you cannot truly claim you mastered the understanding of any business before figuring out what is wrong with it and how to fix it.

Accordingly, in this phase, the key part is to identify and define the problem you are trying to solve. To do so, you first need to **identify the relevant teams and key stakeholders** within the various business units. The stakeholders would not necessarily be those who hold the highest ranks, but rather those who are in the position to drive change through and open enough to do so.

Once you identify them, the next stage would be to **conduct open discussions to better understand their day-to-day operations.** This part is very important since once you are able to identify and define the problem you are trying to solve, you can avoid any preconceptions that you might have.

Then, it is important to **understand and identify challenges and pain points** as part of the product strategy; what are the day-to-day roadblocks, trying to **address blind spots,** to be able to leverage the right technology and know-how in order to accelerate and enrich product enhancement.

Next, the focus should be on **prioritizing and narrowing down** the list of relevant technologies that could be integrated into the core operations of the business.

7.1.1 Identifying the Problem

For a corporate innovation team, gaining traction is one of the most significant hurdles to overcome. By traction, we refer to the ability to push forward and successfully integrate start-ups or collaborations into the product roadmap.

Many teams try to achieve this by utilizing an outside-in approach, where they seek out interesting startups and opportunities and then try to identify the right fit within the organization. However, in my experience, I have found that utilizing the inside-out approach for more established companies is considerably more effective, as I will elaborate on later.

Stephen Covey, in his famous book: "*The 7 Habits of Highly Effective People*," argued that focusing on an inside-out approach is more effective in achieving long-term success and fulfillment for individuals, as it is based on a strong foundation of personal values and principles.[*]

Similarly, I believe that when searching for new technologies externally, depending solely on the outside-in approach during the scouting phase might not be the most effective strategy, particularly for an engineering firm. When it comes to onboarding external solutions, relying solely on the outside-in

---

[*] S.R. Covey. 1989. The 7 Habits of Highly Effective People, Simon and Schuster.

approach can lead to a "solution searching for a problem" situation, which could turn into a waste of time and resources. To avoid this, a more effective way is to adopt an inside-out approach that involves first understanding the company's strategy and technical gaps that need to be addressed. Once we have a good understanding of the corporation's needs, we can then leverage our network to identify the right solutions for the organization.

As previously discussed, the core principle for any successful business development initiative is to first understand the corporation's operations and requirements. This knowledge is then complemented by an analysis of the external market to determine the corporation's position within it. In my opinion, incorporating innovation should follow the same path and the process should start with comprehending the corporation's needs and pain points, followed by exploring the external landscape to identify potential solutions that effectively address them.

By taking this approach, we can ensure that we are not wasting time and resources on solutions that do not address the company's specific pain points. Instead, we can focus on identifying and implementing solutions that are tailored to the company's unique needs and goals. This approach can help in achieving better results and drive innovation within an organization, but naturally should be utilized only when the company has a good understanding of its needs and pain points.

While utilizing the inside-out approach is crucial for effective onboarding of external solutions, achieving a deep understanding of the business unit's needs can be a challenge. The obvious and wrong way to solve this would be to simply ask them. This will turn your team into no more than a "picker in a supermarket" for startups and could be counterproductive and lead to missed opportunities and the wrong match.

Therefore, it is not surprising that many innovation groups that go down this path, struggle to move beyond the Proof of Concept (POC) stage and really achieve the right amount of traction.

In many cases, the corporation leaders or engineering teams do not truly know what they need or mix it up with their own preconceptions. They tend to confuse what they are trying to solve with the solution they have already developed, which might not address the problem at all.

Eventually, if you are part of a corporate innovation team, the business units are your customers. They can explain what they need but might tend to confuse it with what they want. As Henry Ford famously stated, if he had asked his customers what they wanted, they would have said "faster horses." In the same way that Ford understood that people do not necessarily want faster horses but rather a fast, affordable, and reliable way of getting from one place to the other, you need to find out what the business units truly need rather than what they want.

For this reason, my approach was always to ask them what are the problems they are facing and struggling with rather than what are they looking for.

This way it would be easier to identify and define exactly the problem you are trying to solve and find the right match.

There are multiple reasons to why people tend to confuse what they need and what they want and some of these include:

- **Mistaking the current state for a given situation**—It can be challenging for people to break away from ingrained habits and ways of thinking that they have cultivated over many years. As a result, they may struggle to find creative solutions to problems that they perceive as unchangeable or inevitable. This can lead them to accept their circumstances rather than seeking ways to improve them.
- **Not looking at the big picture** and focusing only on what your team is working on.
- **Not understanding customer needs** having preconceptions on what the customer's needs truly are.
- **Mistaking customer requests with your own preconception** when the customer explains what he is looking for, there might be a tendency to "translate" it according to preconception.
- **Ignoring market trends**
- **Focusing on the solution you see** rather than the problem you face.

Peter Drucker put this in the perfect way: "The customer rarely buys what the business thinks it sells him." In this way, if you really want to get positive traction, when addressing business units, or even customers in general, focus on the problem at hand rather than on the solution they are looking for.

Suppose a tool company works on a table saw. If you ask the technical team what changes are required to make the tool better, they may suggest improvements such as a better motor, a new blade material, or a longer-lasting battery. However, if you consider the problem they are attempting to solve, it is to save time for construction workers. Therefore, the question you should be asking is how much time the customer spends operating the saw to begin with. It is unsurprising to discover that most of their time is spent taking measurements rather than sawing.

While asking the team what they require may result in ideas to improve the tool, the real issue you are attempting to address is how to save the worker's time. This could lead to an automated table saw that allows users to upload measurements, like the one designed by TigerStop. By automatically adjusting the saw according to the settings, this solution directly addresses the root cause of the problem and reduces the time spent on taking measurements. As a result, users can achieve improved productivity and efficiency at the job site.

By properly identifying the problem, companies can gain a better understanding of their competition and identify competitors they may have previously overlooked. Blockbuster, for example, may have been able to recognize the rise of streaming services like Netflix and Hulu if they had defined the need they were addressing more accurately. Similarly, Kodak could have acknowledged the shift toward digital photography and Blackberry might have seen the rise of touchscreen smartphones as a threat and taken steps to compete with companies like Apple's iPhone.

In light of this, being able to identify and define the problem you are trying to solve is the most important foundation while trying to onboard a solution, otherwise, you will waste time and resources and find that you are barking up the wrong tree.

7.1.2 Focusing on the Pain Points

One of the defining moments of my career happened during my days at Continental, a very traditional German manufacturer. Many engineers and technical experts in the company were extremely proud of the level of products they have delivered and rightfully so, since the company was at the forefront of technical execution. The feeling was that no matter what the customer would ask them to do, they would always deliver it in the best quality possible. Hence, it was quite challenging to push for external innovation, and the technical experts were always very skeptical when facing a new startup. This was even more intensified while working with the tire group that took extreme pride of being at the forefront of innovation in tires worldwide.

During those days I was part of Co-pace, the startup arm of Continental which was responsible for facilitating and pushing forward external collaborations with startups and one of my responsibilities was to work with the tire division to do so. As you can imagine, it does not get more challenging than that, when you are trying to promote external innovation.

The first meeting that I had with one of the top executives of the tire division went well, but then he stated that "although he does see importance in what we do for the corporation, he will never work with startups, because what could a startup teach a company who has been doing this for more than 150 years."

And you know what, he was right when considering the entire process from start to end, including rubber extraction, curing, and the molding of tires. However, when examining each stage of the process individually, the story changes significantly. While I acknowledged his belief that the process was already optimized, I respectfully expressed my opinion that there were likely pain points and areas for improvement that his team was experiencing along the process. I suggested that by addressing each part of the process, we could identify these challenges and work toward developing solutions to address them, resulting in further optimization and increased efficiency. I was even vain enough to suggest that we compile a list of all these addressable needs, and I will be able to provide in return a list of two startups that are working on each problem we have defined. Naturally, he was very skeptical but still intrigued and therefore was willing to give it a try, promising me that if I was able to do so, we would choose one topic and start from there, with his full backing and funding for a Proof of Concept (POC).

This was naturally a bold move since if this had failed eventually, he could have used this as a justification to cease all potential work with external technologies, but I had the impression that he was curious enough to learn what is out there and would be willing to experiment once he does, even if the POC fails.

The POC did eventually fail since we did not define the right KPIs, but it opened the division to experiment more and when I left the company after two years, they were very much involved in ongoing projects across industry 4.0, smart materials, environmental, and sensor implementation.

This is a great example of why you should always start from the pain points; when you do so, the other side would be more open to listen and experiment, because what would be better for him than a solution for a problem, he and his team have been struggling with for quite some time.

The focus should therefore be on identifying these pain points in the right way by breaking the process into phases and defining exactly what problem you are trying to solve in each phase.

7.1.3 Breaking the Process Into Phases

A company might find it difficult to break an entire process into a few phases. This might be easier in companies that use multiple parts from various sources and trickier for those who use one or two main sources of materials in their process. For this reason, it is always important to know that these multiple layers exist and most likely every step along the way is struggling with its own difficulties and challenges. It is therefore important to understand the entire flow and talk to the right people who could help define the pain points they are addressing in each part of the flow.

It is far more effective to break down the flow into various phases and illustrate how you can contribute to each phase, ultimately leading to the optimization of the entire process, than trying to convince others of your ability to improve the entire process altogether.

Eventually, identifying and prioritizing these pain points of each phase along the process might give you the opening you just need to start working on innovative solutions.

7.2 Phase 2—External Exploration or Scouting

Once you have clarified your objectives, the next step is to determine the most effective approach to finding a solution.

As a business development manager, your ability to identify a viable market, establish key connections, and conduct a thorough search is crucial to your success. Building a reliable network can be incredibly beneficial in this regard. With a strong network in place, you can tap into the expertise of individuals from various fields who can help you explore unconventional solutions that might not be readily apparent.

As mentioned earlier, when searching for external solutions, there are two primary strategies that can be utilized: the outside-in approach and the inside-out approach. By understanding the advantages and limitations of each approach and leveraging your network to access external resources, you can determine the best approach for seeking a solution that meets your specific needs and objectives.

7.2.1 Outside-In Approach

The outside-in approach is focused on responding to external factors such as competition, market trends, and customer demands. It is about adapting your actions and decisions to external circumstances and expectations. When seeking external solutions, this approach involves understanding what is available in the market and locating the right fit in your organization. Therefore, this approach is the most common and easier to follow and is usually executed by innovation teams that lack the right technical know-how.

Imagine a giant jigsaw puzzle; in this way, you are trying to match pieces you find into the missing part and work through an elimination process (Figure 7.1).

The outside-in approach to external exploration is an effective way for companies that are just starting out to understand the market landscape. This approach is particularly useful when a company is still in the early stages of its journey and needs to gain an understanding of what is going on in the market.

Although this approach may aid in concentrating the company's efforts on developing in-house solutions tailored to the needs of customers, it may not always be the most effective way to assimilate external solutions for addressing specific pain points.

When implementing this approach to scouting, this becomes "a solution looking for a problem" and therefore less suitable for a company that

Figure 7.1 Outside-in approach

already knows what it needs. This is due to the fact that you might waste a lot of time and resources until you get a right "hit" and get the business units more and more frustrated along the process.

7.2.2 Inside-Out Approach

As companies grow and mature, they may find that the inside-out approach becomes more relevant.

The inside-out approach is focused on developing a clear understanding of your own values, principles, and goals and then aligning your actions and decisions with them. It is about starting from within and letting those internal values guide your behavior and actions. When applying this approach to external exploration, you should start with self-reflection and understand the operational flow. Then you can identify and define the problem or what you are looking for and only then go external, or outside, to search for a suitable match. Here, since you have defined the need already, you do not need to find an exact match but something very close and work with the external company to make this a perfect match.

This approach is more suitable for engineering companies who basically implement this path during their day-to-day operation; defining what they want to achieve and then executing it accordingly. It is also relevant to more mature companies who already know what they are looking for and are willing to work alongside the external solution to fit it to their exact needs (Figure 7.2).

Figure 7.2 Inside-out approach

As I see it, the outside-in approach, while necessary in responding to external factors, can lead to a lack of direction and purpose if not balanced with an internal focus on pain points and needs. Therefore, just as Covey argued that focusing first on the inside-out approach is more effective in achieving long-term success and fulfillment for individuals, I believe that the same applies to corporations when external exploration is based on a deep understanding of needs and pain points first.

To summarize, there could be three outcomes for conducting external scouting:

1. **Outside-in approach**—starting from an external solution and finding the best fit for it within the organization.
2. **Inside-out approach with incorrect problem definition**—focusing first on the company's needs and pain points but failing to identify and define the correct problem, looking for what is wanted and not necessarily what is needed.
3. **Inside-out approach with correct problem definition**—asking the right questions to identify the problem and focusing on technology gap, transforming startup scouting into technology scouting.

7.2.3 Turning Startup Scouting to Technology Scouting

Many companies, while searching for external solutions, tend to focus on "looking for the coin under the lantern," while still taking pride in their various startup programs.

Collaborating with startups through incubation programs, accelerators, and company builders that specialize in a particular vertical has become a common practice for companies striving to stay at the forefront of innovation. However, the question remains whether this approach is truly the most effective one.

As discussed, when incorporating these programs, many companies struggle on the execution side and find themselves stuck after the Proof of Concept (POC) phase, even if these POCs were successful by every measure.

Ultimately, the real intention of collaborating with an external company is to enrich and accelerate the company's product roadmap, to find new and exciting areas to play in, and be able to compete in the long term with ever-changing business environments.

In an effort to cultivate a more open-minded and challenging internal culture, the corporation may seek to introduce their staff to external solutions and a startup mentality. While this approach can encourage innovation and agility, it may also cause the company to overlook great internal ideas that lack the extra push to succeed.

Therefore, in order not to lose track of what you are trying to achieve, you need to understand that collaborating with external companies such as startups is just one way to become more innovative and the focus should turn from Startup Scouting to Technology Scouting.

It is important to take a step back and assess the situation objectively. Once you have invested time in identifying the problem you wish to solve and clearly defined your goals, you can then shift your attention to the technology that can assist you in achieving them.

Although concentrating on relevant solutions within a given sector may appear to be the simplest approach to take, genuine innovation comes when one turns their attention to the technological need and broadens their search beyond the traditional boundaries.

In this way, when searching for an Artificial Intelligence (AI) solution in a specific sector for example, first figure out what are you trying to achieve and whether AI is even the right approach. Then you can even find a solution from another team within the company or another sector altogether, since it addresses the technological need and could be the best fit to what you are looking for.

The technical solution could then come from internal teams, startups, or even larger corporations, that you as a company would never have thought to collaborate with before.

Remember, that the real focus and aim should always remain the technological gaps and what you are trying to achieve.

7.2.4 Focusing on Other Verticals

To overcome concerns and roadblocks in generating new partnerships, one of the most effective methods is to explore mature technological solutions in other sectors that are distinct from the ones your company operates in. This could only be possible while focusing on the technological gap and what you are trying to solve rather than the solution you are looking for and therefore it is important to first identify the problem and technical gaps that you want to address.

You will most likely find that leveraging a solution from another vertical is somewhat less challenging; the internal business units will be less argumentative, and this will reduce the level of NIH syndrome, since it would make sense, in their minds, to bring know-how from a vertical they know less about, rather than an external company that is competing against them on their day-to-day operation. It is also much easier to engage with a company that has already gained experience in another sector and sees the value you can bring to them in their further exploration.

Moreover, the team would be most likely already used to collaborate with large corporations and would comply with regulation needs like privacy, cyber security, and insurance, which will make the onboarding process go much smoother.

Then it is just a matter of management of expectations and working together to build out a new solution.

One of my most fulfilling experiences in my career involved onboarding a new technology for the tire industry that enabled an environmental solution. As mentioned, as part of my work at Co-pace, I was responsible for assisting the tire division in locating interesting external solutions. One particular solution involved a unique marker that could be embedded into any substance, allowing it to be traced and monitored throughout its entire lifecycle, thus enabling traceability for circular economy.

The challenge was locating such a marker that could withstand the tire curing process, which had proven challenging with existing markers.

In order to address the challenge, I realized that we needed to look beyond the tire industry and leverage the expertise of other sectors. With this in mind, I reached out to a friend at BASF who was familiar with such markers for the plastics industry with the intention to apply the knowledge gained in one sector to the other. My friend pointed me to a startup that had developed a marker for the metal industry that could withstand high temperatures, making it potentially suitable for the tire manufacturing process. Although it was a solution from a different industry with no prior knowledge of tires, it had the potential to be a game-changer.

The challenge was to convince both the startup and the corporation to work together. The startup needed convincing to adjust their solution to rubber, and Continental to work with a startup that had no prior knowledge of the tire manufacturing process. It took some effort, but eventually, we were able to bring everyone on board, and Continental announced its collaboration with the startup and its intention to implement the marker in Continental's tires. Eventually, the project was recognized with an award for "Environmental Achievement of the Year for Manufacturing."

This experience taught me the importance of looking beyond one's industry and being open to learning from what has been developed in other sectors. By leveraging external expertise and knowledge, one can identify innovative solutions that meet his company's unique needs and challenges. It also highlighted the importance of effective communication and collaboration in bringing all stakeholders on board and driving successful outcomes.

7.2.5 Where to Look

If you were able to identify and define the problem you are trying to solve properly, you could expand your search beyond what you know and the sector in which you are operating. This, of course, brings you to the question of how to do so and where to start from.

I would therefore like to share some insights that I found helpful while exploring uncharted territory:

1. **Utilize your current network**

   The obvious starting point would be the network you already have. So, working your way from that point would allow you to expand beyond your current reach. During my career, I always made an effort to know relevant experts in other domains. By doing so, I was able to rely on their expertise when faced with challenging questions instead of attempting to solve problems on my own. This approach has allowed me to minimize the amount of time required for research and education, enabling me to be more efficient and effective in my work. Building and maintaining such relationships as part of your network is therefore quite important.

2. **Business intelligence on competitive landscape**

   Knowing what the competitors are doing is always a good place to start from, since people on your side would be more open to an idea if this has already been explored by the competition.

   It is always a fine balance between just becoming a slow follower to your competitors, to trying things by yourself first, or as a top executive in the automotive world once told me: "I don't like to be first, but I definitely won't want to be second." Knowing what your competition is doing is definitely a piece of an information you need to know about, and besides, if you are not aware of what is going on in the market you are playing in, you are not doing your job properly.

3. **Gaining knowledge from other industries**

   If your company is open to experiment, following trends and opportunities could teach you a lot. These go beyond your current market, and you can leverage the know-how from another sector to educate yourself. This reflects an approach I have always aimed to follow: "When you want to learn something new, don't ask someone who thinks he knows, ask someone that has done this five minutes before you."

   There are numerous examples that demonstrate the value of leveraging existing technologies from other markets. For instance, agricultural companies developing autonomous lawn mowers - learning from the automotive industry, cyber security and radar solutions coming from military applications, computer vision for automotive and industry 4.0 that came from homeland security, virtual reality in healthcare from the gaming world, and self-driving car from the aerospace industry are just a few examples of learning from existing technologies from other sectors.

4. **Enriching current product offerings**

Looking at what you currently have, trying to make it better, does not necessarily fall under innovation but rather in the realm of product enhancement, but it is always a good place to start from, especially when external insights are brought into the mix. A good example would be new materials that could make the product lighter, cheaper, and more durable. A positive experience could just be the first step you need to spark the desire of the business unit to experiment more.

5. **Customer requests**

Gaining insights from customers is crucial, but as discussed, it is important to distinguish between what they think they want and what they genuinely require. By doing so, you may uncover innovative solutions to address their pain points, as demonstrated by the table saw example above. By understanding the specific difficulties customers are facing, you would be able to develop creative approaches to overcome these obstacles and provide effective solutions that truly meet their needs.

One example that illustrates this concept comes from my past experience working with a multinational organization. The company had several factories operating on different systems, making it challenging to gain a comprehensive overview of their operations. At first, they considered unifying all their factories under a single operating system to solve this issue.

However, they later realized that a more practical and effective solution was to adopt a Software-as-a-Service (SaaS) solution that could integrate all the various operating systems into a single dashboard.

In this way, by addressing the real pain point, the manufacturing management (the customer in this case) understood that there was

no need to go with their initial solution and change the entire operating system across all factories. The solution was much simpler; to
rather unify the existing operating systems into one dashboard which
was a far less time-consuming and costly approach.

6. **Utilize external partners for identification and collaboration**
   Many organizations such as university research departments, innovation hubs, Venture Capital firms (VCs), accelerators, corporate
   laboratories, and relevant start-ups seek out the collaboration with
   business corporations and could become a very good source for ideas
   and solutions.

   Being part of a business community or a university alumni
   program is a great resource too, that allows you to tap into a wide
   range of knowledge that is easily accessible and extends beyond your
   current network.

   Although the options mentioned above can be valuable, some
   may not lead to a mature enough solution that can be implemented
   directly into a commercial company. Thus, you will need to treat this
   as a "further down the road" solution rather than an immediate one.

   As mentioned, for short-term solutions you will need to focus
   on either the mature startups/companies in the sector you are operating in, or suitable technologies that could be leveraged from other
   sectors. This might be a shorter path for implementation but will
   require time and resources, nevertheless.

7. **Establishing a relevant pipeline by leveraging a global group**
   The broader and more diverse your group is, the more solutions you
   will find. Many American companies, for example, tend to focus
   solely on the U.S., believing that they could find an addressable solution close to home. This might well be the case, but they are missing
   out on a much more interesting experience and other potential solutions out there.

   In some cases, you might even find a more suitable solution
   because it will be cheaper, easier to integrate, or simply because the
   management is more skilled and willing to adjust to your needs.

7.3 Phase 3—Onboarding

The onboarding process goes beyond simply accepting an external company as a vendor. It involves successfully integrating the company's technology into the corporation's product roadmap, building a partnership, and creating a framework for collaboration. It is therefore the most complex and problematic phase to overcome since it requires the collaboration of many other parties. Being able to orchestrate this process and motivate people to join, would be crucial for the success. By understanding the process and laying out the foundations, you can reduce the frictions and increase the chances of a successful integration.

7.3.1 POC and Beyond

Once you have identified the right company, it is important to understand what comes next. Usually, the next phase would be to evaluate the capability and suitability of the technology you have identified. For this stage, many corporations go through a Proof of Concept (POC). The idea behind a POC is to examine the validity and claims of the company in question; is the technology capable of doing what it claims to do? Once the POC is completed successfully, many corporations move to a pilot or small-scale implementation, where they would collaborate with the external company to examine the compatibility to the organization's needs.

It is very important not to confuse these two phases or mix them together. Seldom does an external company have an exact fit and there should be an integration and molding phase that adjusts the technology to the corporation needs.

Focusing solely on finding exact matches can quickly lead to frustration or realization that you are too late to the game and a competitor has already beaten you to it. So, first set out to examine whether the technology even works; it should be a simple "go-no-go" decision. If the technology works and has the potential of answering your needs, you can then move on to collaborate with the external company into molding their technology to your needs.

The commercial discussions with the external company should be initiated only after the corporation has gained a level of comfort with the solution, which can be established through collaboration during the POC and pilot phases. It is important to evaluate the technology and establish trust before engaging in commercial discussions, as doing so prematurely can damage the relationship and hinder progress. It is similar to proposing a prenuptial agreement on a first date, which can be off-putting and inappropriate. Hence, it is important to progress through the right stages of evaluating the technology, building trust, ensuring it can be integrated into the product roadmap, and only then addressing commercial discussions.

Subsequently, setting the right Key Performance Indicators (KPIs) for each phase is critical for the success of the onboarding process and would avoid frustration or even successful POCs leading to nowhere.

As stated, focusing only on external solutions might cause many companies to become oblivious to great internal ideas that lack the extra push to become more successful, so synchronization with other business units and divisions is also something you should strive for, making sure that some other group hasn't started working on a solution to the exact same problem you are facing.

Remember that this should not be "Startup scouting" but rather "Technology scouting."

As discussed, this could come from internal teams, startups, or larger corporations, that you as a company would never have thought to collaborate with, since they are not a supplier or customer.

Strive to build a strategic alliance that fills in the gaps, either via startup engagements or alongside more mature companies, but the real focus and aim should always remain the technological gaps and what you are trying to achieve.

7.3.2 Setting Up a POC

Setting up a POC might sound like an easy task, but those who have been doing this for quite some time know that this is rarely the case. It takes a lot to align expectations and work on the contractual agreements with legal and procurement, who in many cases might not be experienced in working with a startup.

To effectively set up a Proof of Concept (POC), it is important to understand the organizational procedures involved in the process. In many cases, these procedures are no different from onboarding a regular vendor, which can lead to unnecessary bureaucracy and delays. To streamline the process, it is essential to establish a framework that is accepted by legal, financing, and procurement departments, which will enable a smoother and less restrictive POC setup. It is important to establish a common understanding that a Proof of Concept (POC) is a preliminary step before onboarding a regular vendor. Its purpose is to help filter potential companies better and determine whether they are a suitable partner for the organization. As I see it, it makes no sense to onboard a startup as a vendor before determining whether it is a suitable partner to begin with. Consequently, evaluating startups through a POC should be part of the onboarding vendor process, enabling a fast go-no-go decision and moving on to regular vendor boarding.

This approach makes sense on multiple fronts: the organization has a team to help filter potential vendors and reduce risks, while legal, financing, and procurement departments can assist with the filtering process and reduce resources on their end while minimizing risks. Finally, startups can avoid wasting time and money, which are two of the most critical resources for them.

The question of who should cover the costs of a Proof of Concept (POC) is always a consideration. Startups typically expect the corporation to cover these costs since they have to devote time and effort that is not part of their product roadmap. On the other hand, corporations may feel that they are providing the startup with a valuable opportunity, and therefore, the costs should be part of their marketing expenses.

Although this may have been the case in the past, current-day startups have numerous options and alternatives and therefore are unlikely to engage with a corporation that does not cover their basic costs for the POC. In my opinion, this is one of the reasons why a POC should be kept as simple as possible. The corporation should cover the expense of the time and effort required for the POC itself, and the startup should not see this as a way to earn more money and in return devote their time and effort to make the POC a success.

If the POC is successful, and adjustments need to be made to make it product-ready, additional investment can be discussed on a specific project basis as Non-Recurring Engineering (NRE) or investment into the company.

This approach ensures that both parties are invested in the success of the POC and reduces the risk of misunderstandings and conflicts over costs.

A POC could accordingly be broken down into the following steps:

1. **Breaking Ground**
   I. Aligning mutual expectations of the corporation and the external company you are evaluating
   II. Selecting a corporate champion within the business unit
   III. Providing necessary support and resources
   IV. Allocating budget for evaluating the feasibility of the technology

2. **Setting Up an Operational Framework**
   I. Setting up testing metrics, KPIs, deliverables, and timelines
   II. Defining a collaboration model
   III. Applying a relevant use case
   IV. Establishing governance guidelines
   V. Signing off on regulatory and information security requirements

3. **Measuring Success**
   I. Tracking and monitoring progress
   II. Analyzing results, KPIs, and benchmarks
   III. Assessing the potential and the Total Addressable Market (TAM)
   IV. Building the business case with the commercial teams

Post POC

After the POC has been completed successfully, there should be a much closer relationship between the business unit and the external company. This does not mean you need to step out, on the contrary. Even if you defined this as a point of a handoff to the business unit, it is important to still stay in the loop and make sure things are moving smoothly. Building up the business case and helping the business unit present it to their top management are crucial for the advancement of the engagement and a place that an innovation team could shine at, given their expertise in market analysis. This should also be the point to start involving procurement and legal on the commercial terms. The innovation team can act as a mediator between the two parties, playing a key role in building a strong foundation for a future successful commercial partnership.

7.3.3 Working Alongside Other Business Units

It is important to always remember that innovation by itself is meaningless unless it sticks and therefore it must be connected to a business unit that has the budget and resources to execute it.

You might be part of the innovation group of the business unit or on the corporate level, but working alongside the technical team, sales, and product, is crucial for the success of the onboarding process.

When working with these key stakeholders, it is important to understand their priorities; they are more concerned with the core activities they are leading and much less on the far future. Hence, the far future should be the responsibility of specific strategy or designated Research and Development (R&D) teams.

Many of the people in the business units will not see the value in what you do and would look at this as a disturbance to their day-to-day operations.

Consequently, it is important to focus on what is more important for them and that is why you should spend most of your time addressing core activities. The rest of the time should be mostly devoted to adjacent topics they still see value in, and only a small portion of your time should be devoted to out-of-core solutions. Work on the low-hanging fruit and show your value, or you and your team will be gone very fast.

The additional value sets you should be able to bring to the business unit along the process are:

1. **Quick and Agile**

   From answering e-mails and requests and setting up meetings to follow-ups, the business unit is not set to work in the pace of a startup. The innovation team's support would be essential in this situation, as they can alleviate the external company's concerns and provide them with a sense of reassurance. By taking charge of this process, the innovation team can demonstrate a commitment to ensuring the external company's success and make them feel valued. Moreover, the team's guidance and expertise can help the external company navigate the organization more effectively, thus improving their overall experience. Ultimately, by providing comprehensive support, the innovation team can foster a more collaborative and productive relationship with the external company, resulting in a win-win situation for both parties.

2. **Generating and Helping Establishing Trust**
The business unit will always start from a skeptical point of view, challenging the startup at every step. This is something founders can take the wrong way, thinking that someone is dismissing "their baby" or is just taking them for a ride. So, they might become defensive and take things more personally. Acting as a mediator and facilitating a resolution to a problem can be a challenging but necessary process, much like marriage counseling, but is what it takes to build trust and a future relationship.

3. **Setting Expectations—Internal and External**
One of the key reasons for failure is lack of synchronization on what is expected from each side. There should not be an expectation for things to be obvious, but rather stated clearly and agreed upon by both parties. The innovation team, as a mediator, should be responsible to make sure that both sides are coordinated and are not assuming what the other side is expecting from them.

4. **Starting Small**
Whenever trying to evaluate a new technology, there might be a tendency to rush in and try and get it over with as soon as possible. This tendency brings you to leap ahead when both sides are not ready yet to do so. Think of this as rushing into a wedding after the first date; it might turn out for the best, but chances are it simply will not. Both sides need to get to know each other, build up trust, and learn how to work together. Without establishing the trust and common understanding, the engagement will most likely fail. Therefore, it is crucial to build it right; this does not necessarily mean slow, but rather in phases: first validating the technology, then identifying

a suitable use case, and only then pursuing business engagement. It is important to establish clear and defined expectations at each step of the engagement process, outlining what is expected from both parties and how the next phase will proceed once those expectations have been met.

5. **Supporting and Accelerating Engagements and POCs**

As discussed, setting up a Proof of Concept (POC) is not a simple task. It involves a lot of back-and-forth discussions to lay down the groundwork and establish clear expectations. It also requires external and internal alignment to ensure that all parties involved are working toward a common goal.

In addition, there are bureaucratic elements to consider, such as onboarding to the corporate systems and paperwork, which can add to the complexity of the process. This can easily turn out to be a tedious job that business units would rather avoid and not take upon themselves, so assisting them along the process would help steer things forward, while gaining their gratitude.

Even if you are able to intrigue a business unit, you might find out that they have no budget to execute a POC. This might sound very surprising given the relatively small cost to evaluate a technology, but it is part of how business units operate. As with any profit centers, they get their budget approved in advance and need to run with what they have. So, if they did not set some budget aside for POCs, they might simply not have the money at hand. That is why having your own budget to support in the short term will allow them to participate and evaluate the technology, rather than having to wait for the following year.

However, it is important to try and see if the business unit could participate even in part of the cost just for them to show they have some "skin in the game."

6. **Commercial Experience and Know-how**

A team that has been doing this for quite some time can find themselves even educating the business unit leaders, legal, and procurement in the process and the more these internal stakeholders feel confident in the team's capabilities, the more open and willing to experiment they will become, feeling that this team is reducing the risk of failure along the process.

7. **Synchronization Among Various Teams**

The larger and more established a company is, the more challenging it can be to maintain visibility into the activities of other teams. In some cases, it will not be surprising to even find that a few teams are working on the same solution in parallel, not even knowing about each other. For this reason, mapping innovation activities across business units' various teams could bring a lot of value to all teams working on the same problem. Breaking the silos and enabling this collaboration might be a great added value for a team that promotes innovation across the organization.

8. **Leveraging Know-How From Other Industries**

It is not just the introduction of new technologies and startups from other sectors, but the ability to leverage connections and learn from what is going on in these sectors. For example, if you would like to explore a new SaaS model you can always learn from another company with similar characteristics, even if it is from another sector. Moreover, there is significant knowledge that can be transferred between industries, such as leveraging the development of autonomous vehicles in the automotive sector to create autonomous tractors for agriculture. Similarly, medical applications in the automotive industry can be adopted from the healthcare sector, while image recognition technology developed for homeland security can be applied to manufacturing and other industries.

Being situated at the center of multiple integrations presents a significant advantage, as it enables you to learn and apply knowledge from various industries. This cross-industry knowledge transfer can result in novel solutions and approaches that may not have been feasible otherwise. By taking advantage of this central position, you can remain abreast of the latest developments and incorporate new insights into your work, ultimately leading to improved outcomes and increased efficiency.

9. **Continue Monitoring Interesting Technologies**

Many times, the company would come across a very interesting technology, either during events, conferences, or by chance. In many cases, nothing comes out of these encounters simply because the meeting was held with the wrong people, or the company is not in the right stage to collaborate with. Being able to follow through, watch over, and monitor interesting companies could be the whole difference between being a leader versus a follower, finding that your competitor has been moving along with a startup you were introduced to before.

Eventually, if you position yourself in the right way, you would be in a great place to impact the entire timeline of a product:

- **Immediate term** by synchronizing and facilitating collaborations internally and externally
- **Short term** by enabling and onboarding mature new technologies to support core activities
- **Long term** by supporting and enriching future product road map and innovation

7.3.4 Illustration of the Onboarding Process

Figure 7.3 is an illustration of the onboarding process:

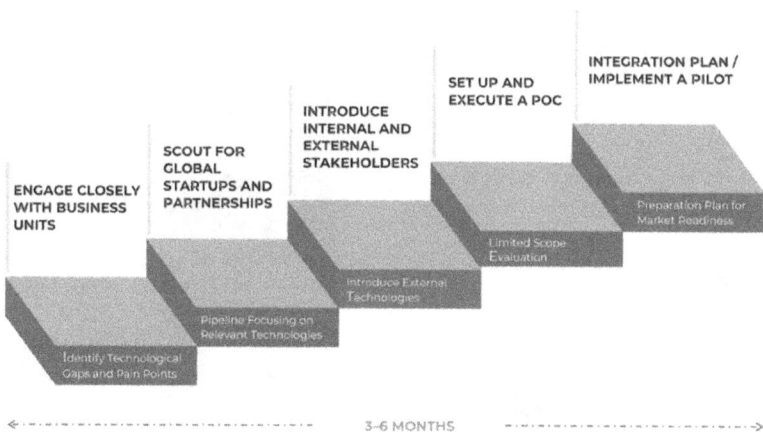

Figure 7.3 Onboarding process

CHAPTER 8

Making It Count— Advancing Innovation

As discussed, implementing new and innovative ideas within established companies can pose significant challenges. These challenges may manifest in negative ways such as Not Invented Here (NIH) syndrome, dismissing the startups capabilities, lack of interest in working with external companies, fear of change, or a general lack of trust. Even if the corporation has good intentions and is genuinely interested in working with an external company, there may be difficulties, such as inadequate processes, lack of vision and clear strategy, treating the external company as a mature vendor, gaps in maturity levels between both companies, or differences in time perception and resource availability.

Despite these challenges, there are guidelines that can increase the chances of a successful outcome.

8.1 Setting the Groundwork

Advancing innovation without laying down the proper foundations is like building a structure without a solid base. To ensure long-term success, it is imperative to prioritize the following fundamentals and build upon previously covered concepts while incorporating new insights:

1. **Establishing Trust and Nurturing Connections**
   Trust is a fundamental element in any relationship. At the end of the day, business is conducted between people, who prefer to collaborate with those they have confidence in. Establishing trust takes time, but knowing what you are stepping into could help accelerate things. Gaining an understanding of the other side's obstacles and concerns is therefore essential. By addressing these concerns strategically at

the outset of the engagement, you can expedite the process. You can do great things when the trust is there, and everything could come to a halt when it is missing. Therefore, it is essential to remain aware and attuned to the level of trust in the relationship. Spend some time to get to know the other side on a personal level before you even start and leave time aside for nonbusiness-related issues. All the big deals that I struck came over coffee or dinner and not in a meeting room.

2. **Management of Expectations**

Failures often occur when both parties are not calibrated and coordinated. It is crucial therefore to establish clear goals, timelines, and expectations for each party involved, to avoid any misunderstandings and ensure alignment going forward. Most POCs or Statements of Work (SOWs) should have very specific indicators to what defines a success or failure and should outline the conditions and timeline for moving to the next step. This clarity ensures that both parties are on the same page and helps to avoid any confusion or misaligned expectations.

It is therefore important to ensure that the other side understands their expected responsibilities and the corresponding timeline for each task. Additionally, it is advisable to have a detailed discussion about contingency plans and alternative approaches to address any potential risks or obstacles that may arise during the course of the project.

3. **Baby Steps**

Taking the time to build a strong relationship is important, and rushing the process can impede its development. By taking small, measured steps with clear definitions of when and how to proceed, both parties can make steady progress toward achieving their goals. While thinking big may seem like a good idea for saving time, it can ultimately backfire. It is important therefore to approach the process in a systematic manner. This involves breaking down the process into manageable and achievable steps that build upon each other, rather than rushing toward the end goal. Although the end goal provides direction and motivation, it is the intermediate steps that pave the way toward success. That is why it is crucial to focus on creating a clear roadmap that outlines concrete and specific steps that lead toward the ultimate objective.

4. **Procurement/Logistics Framework and Support**

It is astonishing how essential this topic is, and yet it frequently goes unnoticed by many companies.

Legal and procurement are the safety guards of the company and therefore it is crucial to bring them on board on what you plan to do, otherwise they can just kill the deal.

If you keep them in the dark about your intentions and plans, they will turn from safety guards to bouncers, not allowing anything to move on unless it falls under their strict rules.

Failing to recognize the unique requirements of onboarding a startup and expecting them to comply with the same rigorous processes as a mature vendor can be detrimental to the engagement. The startup may not have the resources or capacity to meet the extensive requirements of the corporation, potentially leading to a breakdown in the relationship. However, this issue can be resolved by communicating the plans to the procurement and legal teams in advance and working collaboratively to develop a suitable framework. It is essential to acknowledge the differences between startups and mature vendors in the onboarding process to ensure a successful engagement. It is not surprising that addressing this matter is one of the first things I tackle when starting a new position in a new company. This approach has proven to be immensely helpful in expediting the process.

5. **Establishing Clear Handoff Points**

After gaining the support of all internal teams, it is crucial to establish a clear handoff point, which includes defining the handoff process, timeline, and responsibilities to ensure that everyone is on the same page. Even after the handoff, it is important to continue monitoring the project for several weeks to ensure that everything is progressing smoothly, even if it is no longer your responsibility.

6. **Identifying the Right Champion**

As previously mentioned, it is essential to establish a connection with the business units as early as possible and identify an individual who strikes the right balance between seniority and openness to external collaboration. This person should be capable of leading and facilitating the project's progress to ensure a seamless workflow and prevent any oversights. Involving this champion at an early stage can offer valuable insights and help you develop the most effective strategy from the outset.

7. **Defining Achievable Key Performance Indicators (KPIs)**

Establishing clear and achievable KPIs is critical. It is important to set the bar in a way that allows a smooth progression of the POC, with consideration given to what is essential only for a go-no-go decision. It is important to keep in mind that the POC phase is intended to provide insight into the technology's potential and not to identify a perfect fit for organizational needs. Aligning the technology to corporation needs can be addressed after successfully completing the POC and verifying the technology's potential to do so. Setting the bar too high during this initial phase can lead to failure before the project even begins.

8. **Separating Between Commercial and POC Discussions**

Many companies make the mistake of linking the POC to commercial discussions, aiming to ensure that both parties see the relationship eye to eye. While this approach makes sense to some extent, as it ensures that both parties are aligned before investing time and resources, it is not advisable to mix the two. It is better to agree on a high-level alignment, but treat the POC solely as a test to validate the technology and ensure that the other party has what they claim to have.

By collaborating through the POC phase, trust can be established, which can lead to smoother commercial discussions.

Moreover, discussing commercial terms before establishing trust, building a relationship, and confirming the validity of the technology can end up taking more time than anticipated.

9. **Focusing on the TAM**

Many executives or key decision makers in business units are very tuned toward Return on Investments (ROI), as discussed. They think as salespeople (and rightfully so), trying to understand very simply how much will it cost them and what is the expected return. Since many engagements on the innovation front cannot show a clear and tangible ROI very early in the game, simply because it is a new market or business model, they might kill the deal before giving it a real chance. Therefore, it is important to avoid discussions on ROI before the POC stage, focusing on the Total Addressable Market (TAM) first, talking about potential and opportunity. Once the POC phase has been completed successfully and the project has progressed to commercial discussions, addressing the topic becomes more straightforward. With a better understanding of the solution and its potential in the market, the business unit can then engage in more productive discussions.

10. **Working with More Mature Companies/Startups**

As discussed, it is more challenging for a traditional company to engage with an early-stage startup. Traditional companies need something tangible they can play with and often struggle to envision the future without tangible evidence. Hence, it is important not to overlook the opportunity to collaborate with more established companies. By identifying the right partner and defining a mutually beneficial arrangement, it may be easier to gain buy-in for your innovation initiatives and push them through successfully.

By investing time in laying the groundwork in advance and developing strategies for overcoming potential obstacles, you can significantly increase the success rate of the POC and subsequent stages. This approach minimizes the likelihood of encountering unexpected barriers and ensures that the process moves forward smoothly.

8.2 Persistence and Perseverance

Persistence and perseverance are the ability to continue working toward a goal or objective, even in the face of challenges, setbacks, or failures.

It requires resilience, which means having the ability to bounce back from failures or setbacks and keep going, determination, focus, patience, adaptability and ability to always maintain a positive attitude.

Successfully advocating for a topic you believe in, without alienating the other party, requires finesse and skill. As a business development manager, you must leverage all your talents to do so effectively.

Rather than engaging in a confrontational approach on the issues that the other party is currently dealing with, highlight how your collaboration can contribute to their success and help them achieve better outcomes.

This method has demonstrated its efficacy across diverse cultural environments. Convincing a German or Japanese company to embrace risk-taking and experimentation or convincing an American company that they are doing something wrong, can be quite challenging. However, the key to success is to show that you are there to assist them in overcoming their obstacles and minimizing risks.

To achieve this, it is critical to demonstrate the potential benefits of taking calculated risks and establish a comprehensive game plan that allows for a smooth exit with minimal consequences, if necessary. Creating a structured, step-by-step plan can be instrumental in achieving buy-in from risk-averse stakeholders.

In contrast, when dealing with the latter situation, it is essential to avoid highlighting the mistakes of the opposing party. Instead, it is important to acknowledge the strengths of their current approach while suggesting alternative strategies that may yield better results. By focusing on positive aspects and offering constructive suggestions, you can encourage business partners to embrace new ideas and approaches.

One of the key benefits of persistence and perseverance is that they help to build resilience and out-of-the-box thinking. In business development, there will always be obstacles and roadblocks to overcome. By staying persistent and persevering in the face of these challenges, you can build the resilience or come up with a different approach to continue moving forward, even in the toughest situations.

Promoting environmental solutions is a prime example of a key topic that corporations often want to address, but face setbacks during integration. These setbacks can arise due to factors such as a lack of perceived ROI, no current market need, or resistance from day-to-day operations.

Therefore, this topic was typically discouraged as a potential innovation area in many corporates I worked with, due to the significant risk of failure associated with it.

Simply believing in the matter and finding the right solution was not enough; it was crucial to onboard others within the organization to support the initiative. To overcome individual hesitancy toward the topic, it was crucial to identify what would excite each person and motivate them to experiment with solutions. Some were motivated by the potential positive impact on the brand, while others were intrigued by the potential for cost savings. Additionally, others were excited by the prospect of being the first to market with such a solution. By leveraging the power of storytelling and creating a sense of urgency, it was easier to rally support and drive the topic forward in more than one occasion.

8.3 Creating a Sense of Urgency

If things are not moving in the desired direction, you can always take it to the next level and try to motivate the other party by rattling him. Of course, I do not mean physically (although in many cases you would wish you could), but rather try and get them out of their comfort zone. Corporate professionals often prefer their comfort zone and may be resistant to change. In addition to exciting them about the potential of your solution, it is important to make them less comfortable with the status quo. This can be achieved through comparisons to competitors, highlighting specific customer requests, or by explaining the evolving market and advancements in new technologies and solutions. By stressing the need for change and the potential risks of maintaining the status quo, you can increase the likelihood of success.

One effective way to create a sense of urgency and rattle the other party is by tapping into a common psychological instinct known as the Fear of Missing Out (FOMO). It is a feeling of insecurity that arises when people feel that they might miss out on an opportunity or experience that others are having. You will find this to be one of the most efficient ways to push innovation within your organization. Few things keep organizational leaders up at night more than falling behind while the competition moves ahead.

Since this is a powerful tool, it should be used smartly and not too frequently, but with the right dosage as part of a strategical discussion you could really get things moving.

8.4 Leveraging Success Stories

One interesting way of utilizing FOMO is by leveraging success stories. Everyone wants to be part of a success and if they feel that things are advancing without them, they will try to do all that is possible to jump on the driving wagon.

I recall a particular story of a business unit lead who was initially hesitant to work with startups. It was not until he learned of a few success stories with other departments that he became interested and engaged.

This approach is particularly useful when the other party lacks vision. Providing examples can help them visualize the potential and be more receptive to the idea. In a traditional company, the initial response is often negative, with people explaining why the idea will not work. Envisioning how it could work can help persuade them to come on board. However, it is important not to overdo it, as people may not appreciate hearing too many success stories that they are not part of.

CHAPTER 9

Overcoming Barriers

Overcoming barriers in organizations is all about identifying and address-ing obstacles that can prevent you from achieving your goals. These bar-riers can take many forms, such as communication breakdowns, cultural differences, resistance to change, and bureaucratic red tape. Overcoming these barriers requires a systematic approach that involves identifying the root causes of the problems, developing strategies to address them, and implementing those strategies effectively.

There are many commonalities among corporations across the globe, and in this chapter, I would like to address the strategies that I have found most effective in overcoming corporate barriers throughout my career.

9.1 Navigating Within the Maze

Working with, or within a large corporation, could be quite challenging and frustrating. So, here are the important things to bear in mind while dealing with such an organization that might help your ride become more smoother:

1. **Focusing on decision makers**

   Nothing happens within a large organization without the buying of a decision maker. Decision makers hold the power to approve or reject new ideas, projects, or initiatives, and they are the key stakeholders who can make or break a deal, so identifying them and getting them on your side is vital for your future operations. Identifying them is a relatively easy task, even if your company does not have an organi-zational chart; everyone knows who they are. Getting to know them would be the challenging part since their time is quite limited, so working through the people who report to them is the next best thing.

2. The importance of middle management

A common mistake is to concentrate solely on the decision makers and overlook the crucial role of middle management. Such an approach could ultimately prove to be the worst course of action. Although nothing gets through without the buying of a decision maker, it is ill-advised to disregard the managers who report to them. First of all, the decision makers did not reach their position by being naive and are aware that when someone contacts them, it is most likely because they need something from them. Therefore, they may not be keen on providing assistance readily. Moreover, their middle management is the group of people who truly make things happen and execute the decisions of the upper management. However, they also have the power to get things stuck in the system. By going over their head, you might give them the feeling that you do not think they matter, which would just antagonize them in the worst scenario, or merely make them lose interest in the best one, making them turn against you and what you are trying to do.

Therefore, the best approach is to spend some time with these middle managers, get them on your side, and help them push what you need up the ladder, having them approach the decision maker for you. This could prove more effective than trying to do so by yourself, since the decision maker would more likely listen to his own people than to you. Moreover, these middle managers would eventually become decision makers, so think like a business development manager and play the long game.

Unfortunately, I have found myself advocating for this approach in almost every multinational company I have worked with, as it has not been widely adopted. I have learned that it is the most efficient course of action in the long term, as it has consistently proven itself time and time again.

For this reason, focus on building a strong relationship with the middle management, turning them into your advocates. Over time, this will pay off.

3. Meeting face to face

While technology has made it easier to communicate remotely, there are certain benefits that can only be achieved through in-person interactions. Working in a multinational corporation, especially post COVID, brought many people to embrace remote work. However, people still pay much more attention and respect to those who make the effort to meet them in person. This is particularly important when working with business associates from the Asia–Pacific (APAC) region, as they view it as a sign of respect and hold it in high regard.

One of the key benefits of face-to-face communication is the ability to build a bond and generate trust. Meeting someone in person allows you to establish a personal connection, which can be difficult to achieve through digital channels. This connection can help to build a foundation of trust and credibility, making it easier to move forward with future projects.

Another benefit of face-to-face communication is the ability to read body language and nonverbal cues. This information can be critical in understanding the other person's true perspective and identifying potential roadblocks or concerns.

In-person meetings provide an opportunity to brainstorm ideas, ask questions, and work together to find solutions. This collaborative approach can lead to more innovative and effective solutions than could be achieved through remote communication alone.

If you must communicate through long-distance calls, it is important to meet the person on the other side in person at least once. To make the calls feel more personal, start by discussing the individual's interests and use video calls whenever possible.

4. **Managing follow-ups**

Regular follow-ups are essential in ensuring that important tasks and projects are completed on time and that communication with key stakeholders remains consistent. By scheduling recurring meetings and setting clear expectations for updates, you can help to ensure that everyone is accountable for their respective tasks.

Face-to-face updates with team members are highly recommended whenever possible, as this can help to maintain clear communication and ensure that everyone is aligned with project goals. If face-to-face meetings are not possible, it is crucial to make an effort to meet with colleagues on the other side before the project begins. This can help to build rapport, gain insight into what motivates the other party, and set the stage for successful collaboration.

Managing multiple engagements simultaneously requires staying organized and efficient. This means being able to prioritize tasks, delegate responsibilities effectively, and maintain a clear understanding of all project requirements and timelines. It is important to take a proactive approach and assume the lead in the process. This means setting up regular follow-ups and check-ins to identify potential roadblocks and address issues early on, rather than relying solely on others, even if it is their responsibility. By staying on top of a project's progress, you can quickly identify any deviations from the intended course and take corrective action before they turn into major issues. What I learned along my career was that the best way to put out a fire is to stop it from ever starting.

5. Persistence and perseverance

As mentioned above, do not get no for an answer. This does not mean you need to be a nag, but definitely try and try again; get more data on the topic and on the person in front of you and schedule face-to-face meetings to push things forward. However, it is crucial to recognize that persistence is not the same as stubbornness. Stubbornness involves sticking to a particular strategy or belief, even if it is not working, while persistence means remaining committed to the goal and being willing to adjust strategies as needed to reach it.

Throughout my career, I have noticed that people tend to respond promptly when they sense that the other side will continue to follow up until they do. This approach has enabled me to establish strong relationships and close deals, even in situations where success seemed unlikely at first.

In many cases, it may take several attempts to get everyone on board with a particular idea or initiative. Therefore, it is crucial to know how to bounce back from negative responses, regroup, and approach the matter from a different angle. However, it is equally important to recognize when to give up after repeated attempts that have not yielded the desired outcome. Many successful entrepreneurs take pride in their failures earlier in their career and I can relate to that sentiment. Throughout my own career, I have experienced numerous setbacks and disappointments, but I have always viewed them as valuable learning opportunities. I strive to learn from my mistakes and failures and use those lessons to improve my performance and increase efficiency in future endeavors.

6. **From suppressing innovation to embracing it**

In many large corporations, innovation is often viewed as a disturbance that takes away from the day-to-day responsibilities of employees. To overcome this, it is crucial to help people understand the importance of innovation for both them and the organization.

A productive strategy to drive innovation is to engage with your colleagues and gain insight into their interests and the challenges they are facing. This way, you can harness their passion and overcome any hurdles that may be impeding innovation, either from their end or from the organization as a whole. Having them as passive supporters is a good start but not sufficient and it is crucial to work on converting them into active supporters.

In more than a few cases, you might encounter situations where individuals are eager to advance their area of interest, but the organization is the one putting up barriers and failing to recognize the significance of advancing innovation around the topic. In such cases, it becomes imperative to collaborate, gain as many supporters as possible, and push the organization and decision makers to prioritize the matter by comprehending market trends. A great example for this is the significance of logistic optimization. Pre-COVID-19, many managements perceived innovative logistical solutions as disruptive to their daily operations. However, during the pandemic, optimizing logistics suddenly became a critical concern for companies, and those who paid attention to this and their employees who pushed this topic forward were better equipped to weather the storm.

Helping these managers to effectively communicate the story to their executives and gaining sufficient internal support is precisely what is required to facilitate their transition from being passive to active.

Taking a proactive approach to innovation is essential, particularly when working with companies that are focused on meeting customer demands. In such environments, promoting innovation can be challenging, and the company may not prioritize it without a direct request from the customer. Therefore, to drive innovation forward, it is necessary to demonstrate the current market trends, showcase the initiatives of other companies, and highlight the importance of innovation to their customers. Advancing environmental solutions and connected devices to enable future data extraction, are just two examples that illustrate how innovation in key topics can lead to improved outcomes for both the company and its customers in the near future.

7. **Embrace your biggest challengers**

Along my career, I found out that your biggest challengers could eventually become your biggest supporters. It is important to keep in mind that if someone opposes you and your ideas, it is not necessarily a personal thing they might have against you, but rather a reflection of their feelings toward the concept. If someone is passionate about a topic, it means they care about it, and it is just a matter of turning them to see it from your perspective.

Engaging with your challengers one-on-one and showing that you value their opinion can go a long way in building trust and turning them into supporters. When meeting with challengers, I often ask for their guidance on how to handle the situation effectively. By asking for their guidance, they feel respected and included in the process, which can turn them into advocates much faster.

I recall a particular case during my time working for a large car importer for a known Japanese brand. We were trying to launch a new model, but we were not receiving sufficient allocations. After some investigation, I discovered that one of the brand managers was intentionally obstructing our efforts.

The next time I had a chance to fly to Japan, I took the opportunity to invite this manager to lunch. During our meeting, I shared the problem with him and asked for his guidance. He was taken aback by my candor and surprised that I had approached him for help. Nonetheless, he offered valuable insight, and from that point onwards, stopped obstructing our attempts.

8. **Value creation starts after the deal is signed**

Value creation does not end when the deal is signed, but instead, it starts at that point.

One of the key benefits of this approach is that it helps to ensure that both parties remain committed to the success of the deal. After the agreement is signed, it is essential to follow through on the commitments made during the negotiation process. This includes delivering on the promises made, meeting deadlines, and supporting when needed.

Another benefit of this approach is that it helps to build long-term relationships. By continuing to provide value after the deal is signed, you can establish a reputation for reliability and commitment. This can help to build trust with clients and other stakeholders, making it easier to establish and maintain relationships over time.

9. **Having a contingency plan**

The cases where everything goes according to plan are extremely rare within an organization and there are numerous unforeseen events that can occur during the process. By identifying potential risks and developing a plan to address them, you can reduce the likelihood of negative consequences. This approach can help to ensure that your business development initiatives stay on track, even in the face of unexpected events. It is important therefore to set aside contingency plans; for example, if the business unit you are working with has a change of focus or you just lost the internal champion. Have a plan in place and try to anticipate unforeseen circumstances along the process and what measures should be taken to overcome them.

10. **Relationships are formed between people**

It is finally important to recognize that while organizations may initiate partnerships, it is ultimately the individuals within those organizations who form and maintain relationships. It is the interpersonal connections, built on trust, mutual respect, and effective communication, which drive successful collaboration. Hence, it is imperative to prioritize building strong relationships among the people involved to ensure a lasting and prosperous partnership between the organizations.

One example of how to effectively execute the principles outlined above comes from my time working for a large car importer and distributor of a well-known Japanese car manufacturer.

Typically, when launching a new car, the process involves working with the designated country manager to determine the specifications and pricing. The country manager is then responsible for securing approval from their organization. In one case we wanted to import a new model that was not available to our country and the pricing was anyhow too high. Upon investigating, I discovered that the executive manager responsible for the model was the one putting up barriers. I was able to secure approval to meet with him at an event where I knew he would be in attendance. At the event, I introduced myself with a brief statement expressing my belief that our market could become a key player for this model. I then invited him to sit down with me for 30 minutes, explaining that I could provide more information on why I believed this to be true. Although he was intrigued, he informed me that he only had 15 minutes to spare.

Eventually, we ended up talking for an hour about calligraphy and ancient Japanese culture and tradition.

He was so impressed with our conversation that he gave me his personal business card and encouraged me to contact him directly with any needs. After further negotiations, my boss and I flew to meet him for dinner and ultimately closed the deal.

The key takeaway from this experience was the importance of preparation and building a personal connection. By learning about the individual's passion for calligraphy and doing my research, I was able to engage in a meaningful conversation that ultimately led to a successful business deal.

This highlights the importance of preparing for business encounters and how to approach them effectively.

9.2 Business Encounters

Business encounters are essential for building and maintaining relationships with clients, partners, and other stakeholders. These encounters can take many forms, such as meetings, presentations, negotiations, and networking events. Effective business encounters can set the path for the entire relationship ahead and help to establish trust, foster collaboration, and generate new opportunities for growth and development. They also provide an opportunity to share information, exchange ideas, and gain insights into the needs and perspectives of others.

In today's global business environment, where competition is fierce and customers are looking for the personal touch, the ability to navigate business encounters with skill and confidence is more important than ever.

Here are some key insights that have served as my guiding principles for business encounters:

1. **Educate yourself on cultural background**

    Culture plays a significant role in shaping people's beliefs, values, and behaviors. Different cultures have different expectations and norms regarding communication, decision making, relationship-building, and business practices in general.

    Consequently, gaining knowledge of the distinct beliefs, values, and customs that could shape the behaviors and attitudes of people you are about to meet could help pave the right way.

    In certain cultures, for example, such as those in East Asia, business cards hold great significance as they are viewed as a representation of the individual. Therefore, not treating business cards with respect, or not having them at all can be seen as a sign of disrespect toward the other party.

    Learning a few keywords in the other party's language and understanding how to introduce yourself appropriately based on local customs can significantly enhance your interactions and serve as an excellent icebreaker, setting a positive tone for the business meeting ahead.

    By understanding the culture of the people you are about to meet, you can avoid misunderstandings, show respect for their customs, and build rapport more effectively. This, in turn, can help to establish and maintain positive business relationships, which is crucial for the success of any business venture.

2. **Understanding mindset differences**

In multinational business operations, understanding cultural differences and adapting accordingly is crucial. However, it is important to recognize that conducting business with different cultures goes beyond nationalities and extends to the specific group you are meeting with, such as engineers, salespeople, or legal representatives. It is about the ability to comprehend different ways of thinking, reasoning, and problem-solving that are unique to individuals or groups. Just as Japanese businessmen differ from their American counterparts in their approach to business, engineers differ from salespeople, financing, or legal professionals.

To be successful, it is essential to learn about the differences in values and priorities of the other party, to speak their language, and to communicate in a way that addresses their concerns.

Throughout my career, I have witnessed numerous mistakes made when interacting with diverse sets of people or organizations, from startups presenting their pitch to everyone in the same way, to not knowing how to answer basic questions. For example, if a Japanese or German business manager inquires about your company's plans for the next five years, responding that you do not plan that far ahead would not be a suitable answer. While understanding that both cultures place significant emphasis on the process, it is equally important to recognize that the manager is essentially trying to evaluate whether you have carefully considered all the possible challenges that may arise along the way. Effective communication with diverse groups is therefore crucial in avoiding mistakes and misunderstandings in business dealings.

3. **Ask, Don't Talk**

Active listening is crucial when engaging in business negotiations. By paying close attention to what the other party has to say, you create a more open and collaborative atmosphere that encourages them to share their thoughts and concerns. This allows you to focus on their needs and expectations, rather than solely on your own approach. By listening and adjusting your strategy accordingly, you can address their concerns and expectations more effectively, ultimately leading to a more fruitful relationship.

4. **Avoid making assumptions**

There is a phrase that states that "assumption is the mother of all failures." I found this to be very true and many mistakes and misconceptions came from assuming the other side understands and sees things in the same way you do.

Avoid making assumptions and ensure that the other party clearly understands what has been agreed upon. Send out summaries of the meetings and take the time to understand what is important to them, so that you can address their concerns and ensure alignment. Taking a proactive approach and ensuring everyone is on the same page can significantly improve the likelihood of achieving a successful outcome.

5. **Come prepared**

Preparation is key for any meeting. It is important to come prepared, with a clear idea of what you want to address and be ready for any potential questions. Researching the key individuals, you are about to meet can make a significant difference in the success of the meeting. It is always beneficial to know what to expect and what you are stepping into. Proper preparation allows you to focus on the right topics and understand what interests the other side, as demonstrated in the example above.

6. **Read the room**

It is crucial to pay attention not only to what is said but how it is said, following tone, body language, and implied meaning to fully comprehend the message being conveyed. Cultural context also plays a significant role in communication, as customs and expectations may differ from one country to another. For instance, in Japan, the most important person attending the meeting is not the one speaking, but rather the one everyone looks to when a question is asked or answered. Similarly, in Germany and in South Korea, it is common to continue discussions over drinks after a meeting. If someone requests a break, it may indicate a desire to switch to a more informal setting and therefore pushing for a resolution before the break could lead to a less desired outcome.

7. **Setting goals and action items**

If a meeting concludes without any defined objectives or actionable items, it can be considered unproductive as there will be most likely no tangible outcome. Therefore, it is crucial to ensure that all relevant topics are covered and addressed before adjourning the meeting. In the subsequent meeting, it is important to discuss the action items of the previous session, monitor their progress, and evaluate their execution. By doing this, it would encourage the participants to complete the tasks assigned to them and attend the meeting well-prepared.

Eventually, establishing a successful business relationship is all about recognizing the unique needs and expectations of different groups and being able to connect with them on a personal level.

CHAPTER 10

Mistakes to Steer Clear of

Having discussed the strategies and actions required to succeed in a large corporation, it is equally important to consider what actions should be avoided when addressing these corporations.

Reaching Out to Multiple People Simultaneously

One of the biggest turnoffs happens after the corporation understands that the external company is trying to connect to everyone they can within the organization. The external company might see this as increasing the chances that someone will get back to them, but it mostly has the opposite effect altogether. Apart from this being extremely unprofessional, it leads to animosity for the confusion and the time waste they caused. This could become even worse when there is a dedicated team for such connections since everything will go back to them in any case.

This might also happen at a later stage of the engagement, once the external company feels that they are not getting an answer quick enough or that things are not progressing at a desirable pace.

Due to the fact that large corporations are usually multi layered, and a decision is rarely taken by one person, reaching to a decision could take some time.

Instead of pushing things your own way, it would be more effective to work with the contact person from the corporation and figure out with him who else should be brought on board.

A good friend of mine who leads innovation efforts for one of the biggest automotive manufacturers told me once that "there is no problem from my side to kill a deal, so going up to my manager doesn't make any sense, especially since once this is done, I lose interest."

Cold Outreach

A "cold outreach" refers to contacting a potential customer or client with whom you have no prior relationship or connection. It is called "cold" because the recipient is not expecting the communication and has not expressed any interest in the product or service being offered. This type of outreach is usually done through e-mail, phone, or social media.

Cold outreach is not recommended for several reasons: Firstly, just as attempting to reach out to several people in the organization at the same time, it can create a negative perception of the sender, as it may be viewed as unprofessional and a misuse of time. Secondly, the recipient may perceive the outreach as intrusive or spammy, especially if the message is too generic or is clearly not relevant to them. While cold outreach may seem like an efficient way to reach a broader audience, it is more likely to have a negative effect and be ignored, particularly if the recipient receives many similar messages daily. A better approach is to try to get a warm introduction through your network. If this is not possible, take the time to research and identify the relevant person in the organization you are trying to reach, and craft a personalized message for them. This will at least show that you have put in effort and are respectful of their time and needs and will increase the chances to get a response.

Not Tailoring the Message

Failing to tailor the message to the corporate's needs and focus would just make the corporation lose interest. This is equally applicable when interacting with individuals within the company. For instance, if you encounter a representative from a relevant company but they are not the appropriate person to address your needs, it is important to ensure that they understand your message and can relay it to the appropriate team. Rather than pitching your solution to an unsuitable person, work collaboratively with them to identify the right partner within their organization who can communicate your message effectively.

Being Too Generic

Being too generic or vague can lead to a lack of interest and engagement from the other side. Corporations are rarely impressed by people who try to keep their pitch mysterious and vague and do not offer much data. In order to generate interest and encourage further exploration, there are certain critical data points that must be communicated. If you are hesitant to share fundamental information regarding your company, such as what sets you apart from competitors and your unique value proposition, you may not be prepared to engage with other companies.

Coming Unprepared to a Meeting

Failing to review relevant materials and familiarize yourself with the company and people you are about to meet, could have a number of negative consequences. It can feel like a waste of everyone's time, as the meeting may need to be rescheduled or extended in order to cover the necessary information. It can also lead to misunderstandings, as participants may not have the same level of understanding or context for the discussion. In general, people on the other side will most likely view this as unprofessional and unrespectful to their time. This could reflect poorly on you and your company as a whole and could result in a lack of interest to continue any further engagement.

Being too Aggressive

Exhibiting overly aggressive behavior, irritating others, and pushing too hard can lead to a negative impression and a lack of interest in working with you. Therefore, it is crucial to monitor your temperament and behavior, even if your typical business conduct may differ. For instance, in East Asia, losing one's temper can be perceived as a sign of instability and rudeness, and can potentially harm business relationships.

A colleague once said something that really resonated with me: "The more you push, the more skeptical I become."

Behaving Unprofessional

It is imperative to remember that the primary objective of any business interaction is to establish a professional relationship. While it can be beneficial to incorporate personal aspects into these interactions, it is vital to strike a balance between personal and professional interactions.

Inappropriate personal interactions or oversharing can lead to misunderstandings or even harm the professional relationship. Therefore, it is essential to maintain a level of professionalism while still being friendly and approachable. This becomes even more crucial when stepping outside of the conference room and engaging in social activities.

Excessive Self-Promotion

People tend to dislike sleazy salespeople and therefore the most effective way to present yourself is by letting others understand your value without constantly highlighting it. While it is appropriate to discuss one's achievements during an initial introduction, it is crucial to do so without appearing arrogant. Hence, it is vital to strike a balance between promoting oneself and remaining humble. By doing so, one can effectively communicate their worth without coming across as overbearing or insincere.

Not Being Clear and Concise

Failing to communicate clearly and concisely can lead to confusion and a lack of interest and engagement. When people are uncertain about what is expected of them, they may become disinterested and view the other party as unprofessional or unprepared for collaboration. This can ultimately hinder the development of productive and fruitful partnerships. This is why it is essential to articulate one's expectations and goals in a straightforward and transparent manner. By doing so, it becomes easier to establish mutual understanding and build trust, which are essential components of any successful professional relationship.

Incidental Versus Essential

Essential refers to the most important or fundamental aspects, while incidental refers to characteristics or features that are not necessary. I have seen, for example, some startups place unnecessary emphasis on Non-Disclosure Agreements (NDAs), often excessively altering the suggested wording and causing undue delays. Given the fact that these agreements are typically standard and generic, a large corporation may not have the time, willingness, or capacity to engage in alterations and may opt to end the engagement altogether. This is because it raises concerns about the startup's ability to handle more critical challenges if they are expending too much effort on minor issues.

Failing to Understand the Decision-Making Process

A large corporation has its own processes that no one can change, not even for you. It is just their way of conducting business and you will have to learn to respect this. You can however work with the other side to help expedite and try to adjust to the current situation. A recurring example is companies' policies and agreements that are very focused on customers and vendors. So, onboarding as a vendor with all the requirements might not make sense for a startup that is just going through an evaluation of their product. Understanding the basis for such requests will enable you to work with the company to find the right framework after addressing their concerns and sharing your own.

Not Staying True to Your Word

It is important that you deliver upon your obligations and commitments, especially if you promised to do so. Failing to do so could undermine everything you have built and be detrimental to your future relationships. People dislike negative surprises, so it is important to communicate any setbacks while still showing that you are taking ownership of your mistakes and working to resolve them. Keep in mind that trust is built over time but can be easily destroyed.

In conclusion, establishing a long-lasting relationship with a large corporation requires a deep understanding of how they operate, what they prioritize, and what common pitfalls to avoid. By following these guidelines, individuals can avoid making missteps and establish productive and fruitful partnerships with large corporations that endure over time.

CHAPTER 11

Summing Up

There is a direct linkage between innovation and business development and one can become the natural extension of the other if you truly want to incorporate and advance innovation.

While innovation is all about generating new ideas and finding ways to incorporate them, business development takes this to the next level and finds the best approach to integrate these ideas into the product roadmap.

This book laid out a practical guidance on how to achieve this aim and shared insights into how to apply business development principles to innovation incorporation. It covered the development of an innovation roadmap, as well as the challenges faced by both corporations and individuals in implementing innovation.

The book also took a structured approach to business development, breaking it down into building blocks and various phases, while emphasizing its importance to the future development of any given company. It provided a comprehensive understanding of the principles and practices of innovation and business development, making it a valuable resource for anyone looking to drive innovation within their organization.

By utilizing best practices from business development, readers are shown how to advance their innovation efforts.

In this book, I have shared my experience and insights on the innovation process from identifying the relevant problem to scouting for the right technology, onboarding it, and addressing the right partners. The book provides actionable items that are easily adaptable, addressing a variety of readers.

Startups looking to better understand how large corporations operate, business leaders and managers seeking to drive innovation and growth within their organizations, and corporations struggling to prioritize and make decisions on the best path forward will all find this book useful.

This journey toward innovation is an exciting one, and the knowledge gained from this book will be valuable in embarking on it.

As with any journey, it is important to be prepared to adjust as you move forward. Take note of what has been successful, so you can continue to build upon it, and also take note of what has not worked. Learn from these failures and use this knowledge to avoid similar mistakes in the future.

Continuous learning and improvement are essential components of the innovation process. Remember that innovation is all about creating something new, which often involves taking risks and making mistakes. It is through learning from these mistakes and continuously improving that true innovation can occur. While it is important to minimize the risks associated with the innovation process, it is equally important to acknowledge that taking risks is an essential step to initiate this journey in the first place. Trying to avoid risks altogether may seem like the safe option, but it can prevent individuals and organizations from achieving their full potential.

Isaac Newton once said: "If I have seen further, it is by standing on the shoulders of giants." As humans, we have always progressed by building upon existing ideas and developments of those who came before us. This principle holds true in the business landscape as well, and the best way to progress is still to learn from the successes and failures of others.

I firmly believe that embracing external knowledge and expertise is the best way for any company to advance, and it is simply a matter of accepting this and optimizing the process. My hope is that this book will serve as a guide for those who are dedicated to innovation but facing challenges in achieving it. I believe that it will equip them with the tools and direction to turn their ideas into reality.

By sharing our personal experiences and the strategies that have worked for us and others, we can inspire and empower one another to push the boundaries of what is possible. Together, we can create a better future for ourselves and for society as a whole. Let us build upon the ideas of those who came before us and continue to innovate, turning our ideas into reality and creating a world that is more innovative and forward-thinking for all.

APPENDICES

Summarizing Some of the Processes in This Book

Appendix 1—Corner Stones for Business Development

1. Generating a long-term value
   a. New revenue streams
      I. Introducing new products and services
      II. Leveraging existing assets and capabilities
      III. Expanding into new markets
   b. Reducing costs—operations optimization
   c. Corporate social responsibility
2. Customer relationships
   a. Customer discovery
   b. Customer acquisition and retention
3. Market opportunities
   a. Market research and analysis
   b. Competitive analysis and market positioning
4. Partnerships and collaborations

Appendix 2—Business Development Foundations Applied to Innovation Exploration

1. **Starting from within**—Self-reflection and understanding the corporate strengths and pain points before going external. This approach can aid in generating partnerships, identifying additional revenue streams, and pinpointing the appropriate technology for innovation.

2. **Identifying the problem**—Defining the problem correctly involves focusing on what is needed, not just what is wanted. This helps companies identify their market and competition more accurately and anticipate potential threats as well as come up with relevant solutions.

3. **Leveraging other verticals**—Business development involves identifying and pursuing new verticals to generate new revenue streams. Likewise, incorporating the knowledge and expertise of other sectors can foster innovation, leading to novel approaches and solutions.

4. **Partnerships**—Engaging in partnerships is a key element for both driving business development and promoting innovation.

5. **Customer relationship**—Building proper relationships with customers and gaining insights into their needs and preferences are crucial for both future business development and the ability to develop innovative solutions.

6. **Personal network**—Having a personal network is essential for both obtaining deal flow and acquiring new knowledge and skills.

7. **Competitive analysis**—Understanding the competition's strategy as a driving force for innovation involves going beyond analyzing their features and understanding their overall strategies and approaches.

8. **Internal processes**—Although external factors are often given priority, a company can also enhance its margins by improving internal processes just as product enhancement can accelerate innovation.

9. **Internal and external**—In the same way that business development could mostly push for growth in the outside world, innovation is mostly about onboarding external technology.

10. **Technology scouting**—Focusing on the technical need and requirements rather than a specific use case can broaden the scope.

11. **Where to look**—Exploring and analyzing a new market is performed in the same manner.

12. **Focusing on the pain points**—As a way to onboard innovation and promote external solutions as well as explore new revenue streams.

13. **Breaking the process into various stages**—Breaking down the process into different stages makes it easier to comprehend and evaluate the entire process. This approach can be beneficial in business development as it aids in gaining a better understanding of the company's operations. Similarly, in innovation, it becomes easier to persuade individuals of your ability to provide value at various stages of the process.

14. **Baby steps**—In both practices, it is important to move step by step, gaining trust with the external partner and not rushing into commercial discussions, confusing it with the exploration phase.

15. **Building strong foundations**—Before undertaking any project, it is essential to establish the proper process and framework to ensure its success.

16. **Dedicated team**—A unique and designated team to lead innovation and business development engagements.

17. **Profile importance**—The role of an innovation manager requires a unique set of skills, including storytelling, networking, passion and energy, creative thinking, being a people's person, having gut feeling, and so on.

18. **Getting people on board**—Gaining people's support for activities that go beyond their everyday tasks and harnessing their support can pose similar challenges.

19. **Overcoming barriers**—There are very similar challenges and roadblocks to overcome.

20. **Challenges when facing a large corporation**—Large and traditional corporations face the same challenges and difficulties while trying to step outside of their comfort zone and explore new ideas and revenue streams.

21. **Perception**—Both innovation and business development are often viewed as opportunistic functions rather than stand-alone professions that require time and expertise to deliver desired results.

Appendix 3

Table 1.1—Most relevant sections for various readers

Audience	Relevant chapter
Entrepreneurs	4 Why do companies find it so hard to innovate
	9 Overcoming barriers
	10 Mistakes to steer clear of
Business development and innovation managers	2.1 Cornerstones for effective business development 2.4 Building and maintaining a network
	5 Establishing the right foundation
	7 Phases toward implementation
	8 Making it count – advancing innovation
	9 Overcoming barriers
	10 Mistakes to steer clear of
Executives	2.2 Business development versus sales 2.3 Unique qualifications for a business development manager
	3 A company's journey toward innovation
	4 Why do companies find it so hard to innovate
	5 Establishing the right foundation
	6 Different paths to incorporate external innovation
	7 Phases toward implementation
	9 Overcoming barriers

Appendix 4—Crafting an Innovation Strategy

Innovation strategy is essential for achieving long-term success and staying ahead of the competition. A sustainable innovation strategy involves creating a culture of innovation that is focused on delivering value to customers, creating new opportunities, and driving growth.

1. **Defining innovation goals and objectives**—identifying areas of the business where innovation can create the most value, setting specific targets and timelines for innovation initiatives, and establishing metrics to measure success.

2. **Developing the right process**—for generating and evaluating new ideas. This will involve how to engage with customers and stakeholders, conducting market research and analysis and fostering creativity and experimentation within the organization.

3. **Establishing a framework**—for implementing and scaling successful innovations. This may involve developing a clear implementation plan, allocating resources effectively, and establishing metrics to measure the impact and KPIs of innovation initiatives.

4. **Creating a culture of innovation**—that encourages and rewards creativity, risk-taking, and collaboration. This may involve providing training and support for employees to develop their innovation skills, recognizing and rewarding innovative achievements, and fostering a sense of ownership and accountability for innovation within the organization.

Appendix 5—Onboarding Process

1. Setting the groundwork
   a. Setting up the right team (dedicated operational team, CVC, M&A)
   b. Setting up the right process (budget, strategy and KPIs, framework with procurement and legal)
   c. Setting up the right mindset (the backing of the top management and buying from the business units)
2. Phase 1—internal examination into the core
   a. Identifying relevant teams and key stakeholders
   b. Conducting open discussions
   c. Understanding day to day and the flow of operations
   d. Identifying challenges and pain points along the way
      I. Identifying and defining the problem you are trying to solve
      II. Breaking the process into small phases
      III. Identifying and focusing on the pain points along the way
   e. Prioritizing and shortlisting relevant technologies that could address the needs
3. Phase 2—external exploration
   a. Choosing inside-out or outside-in approach
   b. Focusing on the technology rather than the use case
   c. Identifying where to look
   d. Filtering and prioritizing the findings
4. Phase 3—onboarding
   a. Proof of concept
      I. Setting the POC in place
      II. Formulating an operation framework
      III. Measuring success
   b. Working alongside the business units
   c. Post POC—next stages
   d. Staying in the loop
   e. Persistence and perseverance

About the Author

Yaron Flint is an accomplished business development and innovation expert with nearly two decades of experience in global consulting firms, private equity companies, and leading operational roles in multinational corporations worldwide.

He specializes in implementing innovation within large corporations across various sectors such as Automotive, Industry 4.0, Smart Materials, Environmental, Construction-tech, and Agri-tech.

Yaron's unique cross-cultural and cross-sector experience has provided him with valuable insights into the most effective means of incorporating innovation across organizations. In his book, he shares personal stories from his past experience, expertise, and practical tools and strategies for successfully implementing innovation through business development. Whether you are an entrepreneur seeking to expand your knowledge of the corporate world, a business development manager looking to refine your skills, or an executive committed to driving innovation within your organization, Yaron's insights and experience provide invaluable guidance for successfully implementing innovation to achieve business success.

Index

www.ingramcontent.com/pod-product-compliance
Lightning Source LLC
Chambersburg PA
CBHW061327220326
41599CB00026B/5069